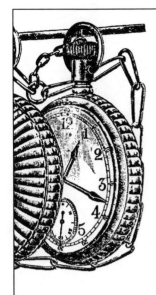

Second Shift

TEACHING WRITING TO WORKING ADULTS

Kelly Belanger
Linda Strom

BOYNTON/COOK PUBLISHERS
HEINEMANN
PORTSMOUTH, NH

Boynton/Cook Publishers, Inc.
A subsidiary of Reed Elsevier Inc.
361 Hanover Street
Portsmouth, NH 03801–3912
http://www.boyntoncook.com

Offices and agents throughout the world

The author and publisher wish to thank those who have generously given permission to reprint borrowed material:

Portions of "Teaching on 'Turns': Youngstown State University's Writing Courses for Working Adults" originally appeared as "Teaching On 'Turns': Taking Composition Courses to a Union Hall" in *The Writing Instructor*, Vol. 15.2: Winter 1996; and as "Critical Literacy and the Organizing Model of Unionism: Reading and Writing History at a Steelworkers' Union Hall" in *Radical Teacher*, 51, Summer 1997. Used by permission of the editors.

Library of Congress Cataloging-in-Publication Data
Belanger, Kelly.
    Second Shift : teaching writing to working adults / Kelly Belanger, Linda Strom.
        p. cm.
    Includes bibliographical references.
    ISBN 0-86709-449-4
    1. English language—Rhetoric—Study and teaching. 2. Report writing—Study and teaching. 3. Adult education. I. Strom, Linda. II. Title.
PE1404.B44 1999
808'.042'0715—dc21   98-51287
                                                                                                      CIP

Editor: Lisa Luedeke
Production: Elizabeth Valway
Cover design: Joni Doherty Design
Manufacturing: Deanna Richardson

Printed in the United States of America on acid-free paper
03 02 01 00 99 DA 1 2 3 4 5

Contents

Part Three: Union-Based Programs

Acknowledgments

We began this project with encouragement from our colleague Virginia Monseau, who first helped us envision a book on writing instruction for working adults. We gratefully acknowledge her wise guidance in prompting us to share what we learned from the adult students we had the privilege to teach. Thanks also to the students whose work and ideas appear in this book, including Denise Sigler, Dan Leihgeber, Cheryl Ross, Anna Maldanado, Amanda Lather, Alan Hearn, Tim Fitch, Rex Raub, Dennis Brubaker, and Barry Frommelt. These students, along with others who took courses at the Steelworkers' Local 1375, have shaped our perspectives on adult-oriented writing programs in important ways.

Numerous teachers and administrators freely shared with us their time, materials, and knowledge about teaching college writing to working adults. We sincerely appreciate the contributions of Jan Kotwis, John Russo, Allison Fraiberg, Donna Shaeffer, C. Alton Robertson, Michelle Burroughs, Mike Kraft, Lucille Sansing, Ruth Needleman, Doug Swartz, Cathy Iovanella, Elaine Handley, Susan Oaks, Cathy Copley-Woods, Herbert Shapiro, Emily Schnee, Silvia Chelala, Jim Robinson, Barbara Kantz, Evelyn Wells, Cara Murray, Norah Chase, Lucienne Muller, Paul Mishler, Sean Sweeney, and Greg Mantsios. Thanks also go to other colleagues, friends, and editors for their time, energy, and support, especially Tom McCracken, Mindy Wright, Sherrie Gradin, Bill Mullen, Rick Shale, Andrea Lunsford, Ira Shor, Peter Stillman, and Lisa Luedeke. Their willingness to read early drafts of the chapters and share their insights kept us moving forward. Generous research support came from Youngstown State University through Research Professorship leaves and two University Research Council Grants. In addition, we could not have finished the book in a timely manner without the indispensable help of our research assistant, Bill DeGenero. We would like to thank *Radical Teacher* and *Writing Instructor* for printing earlier versions of Chapter 7.

Finally, we appreciate the support, advice, and inspiration of Philip Brady and Gary Fetter. They helped in ways too numerous to list—from brainstorming and proofreading, to providing food and laughter, to understanding when our often time-consuming collaborative writing process stretched into a "second shift." Linda Strom dedicates this book to Philip Brady and to her parents, Bill and Jean Rambo. Kelly Belanger dedicates this book to her husband, Gary Fetter, and to her parents, Janice and Larry Belanger.

Introduction

Higher education in the twenty-first century will, in one form or another, increasingly extend itself to provide programs in response to workers' personal, spiritual, and civic needs.
—Shirley Brice Heath,
*Composition in the Twenty-First
Century: Crisis and Change*

Throughout the twentieth century, the project of educating working adults has been embraced by a diverse range of groups and institutions, from informal lyceums and women's clubs, to community colleges, labor unions, and the nation's most prestigious universities. Yet formal education for adults has often been marginalized, seen as the province of continuing education rather than college-credit courses. Although the split between continuing education and "regular" college courses persists today, state schools experiencing dwindling enrollment now compete with new "virtual" universities in efforts to enroll adults, who are quickly becoming the most sought after group of potential college students.[1] Institutions that offer advantages such as flexibly scheduled courses, workplace-based degree programs, credit for life experience, and Internet-based distance learning courses to attract working adults find themselves on the cutting edge of a rapidly changing educational landscape.[2] As writing teachers who have designed and implemented a union-based program adapted to the needs, goals, and experiences of working adults, we see both exciting challenges and cause for critical reflection in the trend in higher education toward accommodating the needs of adult worker-students.

The purpose of this book is to broaden awareness of the exciting pedagogical innovations and adaptations taking place in college and university writing classes designed specifically for working adults. Through case studies of five well-established writing programs for adults, the book is intended to (1) provide a historical context for today's college-credit writing programs for working adults, (2) illustrate a range of accommodations to the needs of adult students, (3) explore how writing programs for adults are influenced by institutional contexts, faculty ideologies, and other factors, (4) inspire in teachers and administrators of adult programs a self-reflective stance toward writing instruction, (5) disseminate innovative teaching ideas, and (6) spur further research on teaching writing to adults.

Our research will especially interest university, college, and community college writing teachers who work with returning adult students, but the chapters of this book are also relevant to any teachers of writing interested in critical pedagogy, writing across the curriculum, community outreach, alternative modes of delivering writing instruction, and connections between composition theory and practice.

Background and Research Questions

The research questions behind this study grew out of our own experiences teaching at a steelworkers union hall and accounts of radical pedagogies in the labor colleges of the 1920s and 1930s, especially Brookwood Labor College and the Bryn Mawr Summer School for Women Workers. Studies on writing instruction at Brookwood and Bryn Mawr by composition scholars Karyn Hollis and Susan Kates immediately attracted our attention since many students in these colleges were, like our own students, industrial workers. Brookwood was a private college in New York open only to unionized industrial workers. The school's mission was to educate students to become active agents for social change, and writing instruction played a significant role in developing the analytical and communicative abilities workers would need to participate in efforts to enact change in their workplaces or in society. Similarly, the Bryn Mawr Summer School relied upon writing instruction to help women workers look critically at their lives and imagine ways to transform oppressive conditions. For Hollis and for Kates, the writing pedagogies at the labor colleges strongly resemble the method of critical literacy education first introduced to the United States in the 1970s by Brazilian educator Paulo Freire (1970b) through his book *Pedagogy of the Oppressed.*

Prompted by the connection between Freirean critical literacy and the history of writing instruction for adults, we initially wondered to what extent present writing programs for working adults represent a Freirean approach to teaching critical literacy.[3] To answer this question, we conducted qualitative interviews and analyzed classroom materials from writing teachers in union-based programs (i.e., programs developed in cooperation with union leaders) and corporate-identified programs (i.e., programs within institutions that seek educational partnerships with corporations through customized courses and degrees). From the data, we found that as a group, the teachers we interviewed share a commitment to teaching students more than simply functional literacy. That is, they all advocate a kind of critical literacy that for each of them involves reflective, analytical reading, thinking, and writing processes that go beyond receiving and understanding information to questioning and testing assumptions. This baseline definition of critical literacy is complicated by theories of composition each teacher brings to the writing classroom. While we realize no teacher's pedagogy can fit neatly into any one theoretical category, we use the terms cognitivist, expressionist, rhetorical, and activist to describe the approaches to teaching critical literacy employed by the teachers in this study. In the chapters that follow, we show how teachers of working adults from past and present programs teach critical literacy filtered through a variety of theoretical perspectives, thus providing a range of models for fashioning effective writing programs for working adults.

Preview of the Chapters

In Part 1, we begin our discussion of writing instruction for working adults by exploring the historical context for current college and university programs affiliated with corporations and unions. Chapter 1 catalogues forms that adult literacy education took in the nineteenth and early twentieth century. Beginning with the mechanics institutes of the nineteenth century, we discuss how the founders' goals reinforced the American ideology of individual self-improvement and social mobility. As unions became stronger, they began developing their own literacy programs and forming partnerships with left intellectuals that led to a more radical approach to workers literacy education. We show how this more radical approach reached a peak in the labor colleges of the 1920s and 1930s, after which the labor colleges began to lose support from unions and universities.

The historical section of the book continues in Chapter 2, where we trace a trend toward vocationalism in literacy education for workers during the 1940s and 1950s. During this time, the onus for literacy instruction for working adults fell to the growing number of community colleges, where adult students were frequently tracked into vocational curricula where writing instruction focused on basic skills. We conclude by discussing how the trend toward vocationalism was disrupted in the 1960s as unions and universities began working cooperatively to develop liberal arts-based programs for workers.

In Part 2, our focus shifts to examine writing instruction for working adults in two corporate-identified programs founded in the 1970s: Alfred North Whitehead College of the University of Redlands and

Empire State College. Chapter 3 examines how the needs of businesses and working students have influenced Whitehead's liberal arts-based curricula. We focus on two writing-intensive courses that give life experience credit and a first-year writing course for business and management students. In Chapter 4, we examine the varying approaches to teaching academic discourse at three Empire State College sites, including the Center for Distance Learning. This chapter shows how Empire State faculty employ a range of writing pedagogies from a feminist expressionistic pedagogy for business executives to a cognitivist approach for distance learning students.

Part 3 analyzes union-based writing programs at Queens College, Swingshift College at Indiana University Northwest, and Youngstown State University. Chapter 5 describes writing instruction in the Worker Education Program at the Queens College Extension Center in Manhattan. We discuss how teachers employ an activist critical literacy through assignments that integrate problem posing, critical analysis, and community action. A similar emphasis on social activism characterizes the pedagogies at Swingshift College, the subject of Chapter 6. In this chapter, we show how a philosophy of writing instruction is still evolving at Swingshift as a writing instructor explores ways to refine an expressionist writing pedagogy within a program focused on social and political activism. In Chapter 7, we describe a developing rhetorical approach to teaching three interdisciplinary writing courses to unionized steelworkers. The Conclusion offers recommendations for developing innovative delivery methods and pedagogies in response to the needs of working adult students.

From the labor colleges to current adult-oriented programs, we found a range of institutional contexts that encourage administrators, faculty, and students to resist traditional models of education. While colleges and universities catering to traditional students often rely on standardized test scores and high school GPAs to make admission decisions, adult-oriented programs adapt admission requirements to consider the value of adults' experiential learning. In traditional college classrooms, students encounter a range of pedagogies from lecturing to more student-centered approaches; programs for working adults also offer a mix of pedagogical styles but faculty across the board value students' experience and even collaborate with students in designing degree programs, curricula, and classroom assignments.

Especially in union-based programs, writing instruction frequently relies on critical pedagogies that challenge status quo thinking through reading and writing assignments that examine controversial educational and social issues. While corporate-identified programs take a less radical approach to teaching writing, in their own ways, they also craft resistance. We found, for example, teachers who resisted reified notions of academic discourse through incorporating into the writing classroom texts representing a range of sociocultural literacies. Altogether, the forms of resistance represented in these programs break stereotypical ideas about adult literacy education as a skill-and-drill process. Instead of reinforcing negative stereotypes, the teachers and administrators in the pages that follow demonstrate the role writing instruction for working adults plays in fostering the critical literacies necessary for a vital democratic society.

Notes

1. In "Collegiate Life: An Obituary," Arthur Levine and Jeanette S. Cureton cite the increasing number of nontraditional undergraduate students who attend college while juggling the demands of work and family: "Currently, fewer than one in six of all undergraduates fit the traditional stereotype of the American college student attending full time, being 18 to 22 years of age, and living on campus" (1998, 14). For more detail about the changing demographics of college students see the 1997 U.S. Department of Education, National Center for Educational Statistics, *Digest of Education Statistics* (NCES 98-015) (Washington, D.C.: U.S. Government Printing Office).

2. As a recent brochure advertises, Phoenix has become "the second largest private university in the country, enrolling more than 25,000 students a year from a growing network of 47 campuses and learning centers located throughout the United States."

3. Currently, Robert Sommer's (1989) *Teaching Writing to Adults* provides the only extended study that draws upon composition research to examine the important role of teaching writing in adult education. His application of composition theory to andragogy ("the art and science of teaching adults") offers useful classroom activities appropriate for adult students. Sommer's teaching strategies are based on methods for assessing adult students' cognitive abilities, de-emphasizing what we see as the important role of social and cultural factors in literacy. Our data allowed us to extend his study because our case studies represent a wider variety of theoretical bases for teaching writing to adults.

Chapter One

From Self-Improvement to Class Consciousness
The Early Roots of Workers Education, 1820–1935

An education which acknowledges the full intellectual and social meaning of a vocation would include instruction in the historic background of present conditions; training in science to give intelligence and initiative in dealing with material and agencies of production; and study of economics, civics, and politics, to bring the future worker into touch with the problems of the day and various methods proposed for its improvement.

—John Dewey,
Democracy and Education

In *Democracy and Education*, written in 1916, John Dewey argues that for working people to participate fully in a democratic society, the nation's approach to education must be reexamined. He critiques the nation's schools for offering upper-class citizens a liberal education that prepares them to take on positions of power while training the poor and members of the working class for manual labor. For Dewey, workers in a democratic society need both vocational training and access to a liberal education steeped in "economics, civics, and politics" so that "future workers would not become blindly subject to a fate imposed upon

1

them" (1916, 328). To some degree, Dewey's ideals have been realized outside the formal school system through two strands in the history of education for U.S. workers: in the early nineteenth century, lyceums and mechanics institutes taught workers the scientific principles behind their work; in the 1920s and 1930s, the labor colleges exposed workers to economic and political thought.

In this chapter, we explore the differing ways in which these two strands of workers education viewed literacy education. Because approaches to literacy education of the past often emerge reconstituted in the present, understanding the roots of education for working adults offers valuable insights into current practices. This history of literacy education for workers provides a foundation for understanding the ideologies and pedagogies that have shaped current programs for working adults. Like current writing programs for workers, the worker education programs of the past reflect the ideologies of their founders, the faculty, the institutions with which they are associated, and the political climate of the country.

Self-Improvement and Upward Mobility: Mechanics Institutes, Lyceums, and Women's Clubs

The characteristically American ideology of individual self-improvement and upward mobility permeate even the earliest roots of U.S. worker education, from the colonial apprenticeship programs and lyceums to the mechanics institutes that flourished in the 1820s and 1830s. Downplaying the significance of social class distinctions, mechanics institutes and lyceums derived much of their popularity from their participants' belief that knowledge, combined with hard work, would result in continual social and economic progress for both individuals and the nation (Sinclair 1974, 10–11). Despite a paucity of detail about literacy education in lyceums and mechanics institutes, we begin our history of teaching writing to workers with these institutes because we see in their ideology a precursor to a still dominant approach to literacy education. As Jim Berlin argues, "literacy for a meritocracy"—that is, a seemingly apolitical approach to education that emphasizes knowledge and skills as the key to success in a capitalist society—continues to compete for dominance in literacy education for workers (1987, 36).

Apprenticeship programs in the early 1800s included a "smattering of general education" in addition to training workers in trade skills. When a variety of mechanics institutes sprang up between 1824 and

1865, they offered more developed education programs by making available reading rooms, libraries, and lectures to teach master craftsmen, journeymen, and apprentices "the scientific principles behind their vocations" and "the values of hard work and social mobility" (Altenbaugh 1990, 22). Although some members of the mechanics institutes argued for participatory approaches to education, mechanics institutes mainly used a lecture-based pedagogy designed to give workers efficient access to scientific knowledge (Sinclair 1974, 109). Perhaps because this "banking approach" didn't require proficiency in reading and writing beyond basic functional skills, little reading and writing instruction took place in these early attempts to educate workers.

Like the mechanics institutes, the lyceums provided citizens another vehicle for self-improvement, providing them with access to lectures on a number of scientific and philosophical topics. Labor historian Richard Altenbaugh notes that some lyceums offered to teach reading and writing along with informal instruction in amusements such as music, gymnastics, and dancing (1990, 23).[1] However, any informal writing instruction offered through the lyceums may not have been available to the class of U.S. workers most in need of basic literacy education to increase their opportunities for upward mobility: a growing sector of working-class people including recent migrants from farms to cities, semiskilled and unskilled immigrants, free blacks, and women in domestic service and craft trades.[2] Although the reformers and entrepreneurs who founded the lyceums and mechanics institutes were driven by idealistic and democratic goals of making education freely available to workers of all social classes, in reality, these early educational movements most effectively facilitated upward mobility for male skilled workers.

For working women of the late nineteenth and early twentieth century, an educational opportunity similar to those the lyceums and mechanics institutes offered men were the burgeoning number of women's clubs. These clubs, described in Anne Ruggles Gere's *Intimate Practices*, "offered members opportunities to develop and enact literacy practices that demonstrated their capacities as writers and public speakers" (1997, 235). As Gere argues, the clubs cut across ethnic, racial, and class lines, offering working-class women a chance to reverse stereotypes that represented "working girls" as stupid and illiterate. Through changing these stereotypes, women developed stronger self-identities and viewed literacy as a way of improving "the material conditions of their lives" (1997, 26). While the women were partially motivated by the desire for self-improvement and upward mobility like their male counterparts in the mechanics institutes, they also viewed literacy as a means of taking action to help change oppressive working conditions. According to Gere, working-class club members wrote papers on child labor, low-income housing conditions, and the disparity between men's and women's wages. They published their writing in the *Club Worker*, a newspaper read by club members throughout the country, and made presentations at conventions for the National League of Women Workers (1997, 26, 235). In their politicizing of literacy, these women's clubs anticipated a trend toward a more radical view of literacy education for working people, a view that culminated in the labor colleges.

Raising Class Consciousness: The Labor Colleges

With the exception of working-class women's clubs, worker education was mostly synonymous with adult education until the first U.S. labor colleges were established. That is, educational opportunities such as lyceums and mechanics institutes were intended for any adult interested in self-improvement and enhanced cultural life. Whereas adult education appealed to the individual worker, movements known as "workers education" focused on the goal of seeking "to make [the working class] self-conscious as an economic, political and social group" (Hansome 1968, 43). With the shift to workers education, literacy education became infused with a more radical ideology. Rather than emphasizing education as a vehicle for individual upward mobility, this "second wave" of education for workers emphasized education—and writing in particular—as a means for working collectively to enact social change.

Even before formalized courses of study became available to selected workers through the labor colleges, literacy education was grafted to the larger Socialist project of raising class consciousness. The Socialist Party and the International Workers of the World (IWW) sponsored study circles, lyceums, pamphlet distribution, book sales, and schools for youth (Altenbaugh 1990, 27–32). These Socialist educational efforts of the early 1900s succeeded to the degree that they attracted support from workers such as the Russian Jews, Germans, and Finnish immigrants who brought Socialist ideologies with them from their own countries. Because Socialist education depended on the participation of immigrants, much Socialist-sponsored literacy education took the form of instruction in English as a second language.

A more ambitious Socialist education project, New York City's Rand School of Social Science, was founded by radical immigrant workers, middle-class intellectuals, and a wealthy benefactor. Although the school attracted many workers primarily interested in a liberal education, the ultimate goal of the Rand School and other Socialist-sponsored workers education was to foster socialist ideas (Hansome 1968, 310). While labor historians never mention writing instruction in accounts of the Rand School, they point out that the school's faculty eschewed lecture-based instruction and introduced participatory pedagogies. Their "question and answer periods" seem to anticipate the Freirean dialogic teaching methods that are essential to developing critical literacy.

As socialist ideas gained currency and influenced workers education, trade union activists also took up the cause of educating workers, emphasizing the connection between well-educated workers and effective union membership. The National Women's Trade Union League (NWTUL), founded in 1903, made education—including writing instruction—a dominant focus beginning in 1914 when they established Chicago-based training schools for women organizers. These schools featured course work similar to that eventually offered by the labor colleges, including classes in "economics, history, and labor problems" as well as "public speaking, drafting trade union agreements, running meetings, union administration, English, bookkeeping, and typing" (Wertheimer 1981, 18). Women also received scholarship money to enroll in college-credit courses from Chicago-area universities. Perhaps because of the training schools' strong affiliation with universities or because the union needed strong writers who could produce effective newspaper articles and reports, these schools gave women extensive practice in writing. Another women's union, the International Ladies Garment Workers Union (ILGWU), which "represented one of the strongest socialist bastions within the AFL [American Federation of Labor]," provided writing instruction through "Unity Centers" that provided courses in English, "psychology, literature, American history, trade unionism, music appreciation, health, and physical education" (Altenbaugh 1990, 34).

The early efforts of the unions and Socialist Party to educate workers culminated in the 1921 First International Conference on Workers' Education. From this conference emerged the Workers' Education Bureau (WEB), which served as a national resource center for teaching materials and publicity. The bureau's founders also imagined that their organization would provide common ground to negotiate the growing tension between trade unionists and socialists. While initially the Socialist Party and labor leaders often cooperated to establish education for workers, a conflict eventually developed between the party's ultimate goal of social revolution and prominent labor leaders' desire to work within the capitalist system to improve wages and working conditions. WEB temporarily united these two groups and paved the way for bold experiments in workers education including the Work People's College, the University of Wisconsin School for Women Workers, and the Commonwealth College. Two of the most notable workers education programs were the Brookwood Labor College and the Bryn Mawr

Summer School for Women Workers, both of which included curricula that relied heavily on writing instruction to achieve its activist goals (Altenbaugh 1990, 38–39).

Brookwood Labor College

In 1921, Brookwood opened the doors of its Katonah, New York, campus to selected students who had "worked in industry and held membership in a labor union for at least one year" (Hansome 1968, 69). This minimum requirement for admission to Brookwood reflects the school's commitment to educating workers for the labor movement. Brookwood's founders, William and Helen Fincke, were Pacifists and advocates of John Dewey's philosophies of democratic education. Through sponsoring a conference, the Finckes enlisted the help of trade unionists, radicals, teachers, and prominent Socialists to transform their preparatory school for working-class children into a labor college for working adults (Altenbaugh 1990, 71). Conference participants published in the *New York Times* the following list of assumptions that inspired the founding of Brookwood:

> First—That a new social order is needed and is coming—in fact, that is already on the way.
> Second—That education will not only hasten its coming, but will reduce to a minimum and perhaps do away entirely with a resort to violent methods.
> Third—That the workers are the ones who will usher in the new social order.
> Fourth—That there is immediate need for a workers' college with a broad curriculum, located amid healthy country surroundings, where the students can completely apply themselves to the task at hand. (Quoted in Altenbaugh 1990, 71)

In a subsequent statement that also appeared in the *New York Times,* Brookwood's founders emphasized that their goal was not to produce labor bureaucrats or ivory tower intellectuals who had been educated "out of their class" (Hansome 1968, 204). Rather, the core of their mission was to educate students to become active agents for social change. Toward this end, the school's teachers and administrators developed a student-centered, class-conscious curriculum informed by Dewey's progressive educational philosophies.

In *Democracy and Education* (1916), Dewey stresses the need for workers education to be more than just vocational training and urges educators to adopt experiential, cooperative, and dialogical pedagogies. Brookwood's faculty applied Dewey's methods effectively throughout a series of courses that sought to empower oppressed or disenfranchised workers to take transformative action, especially through their unions.[3] Courses that sought to develop practical leadership skills included Trade Union Organization Structure, Government and Administration of Trade Unions, Public Speaking, Labor Journalism, Training in Speaking and Writing, and Labor Dramatics. On the other hand, more theoretical courses such as Advanced Economics and Foreign Labor History sought to give workers the kind of broader worldview necessary to imagine and shape their own futures. This combination of practical and theoretical courses reflects Dewey's argument that working people must acquire the intellectual resources gained from studying economics, history, philosophy, literature, art, and science to "share in social control" and "to become masters of their industrial fate" (1916, 330).

Brookwood faculty sought to empower students not only through course content but also through a democratic teaching process. Faculty relinquished many traditional forms of power and control: They did not give letter grades, tests, or diplomas, and students could "dismiss" faculty whose teaching methods were ineffective. Altenbaugh quotes this amusing anecdote about a student's reaction to a prominent economics professor's boring lecture style: "'We yawned as he played around his subject, stalling for time. No salt to his meat. No tang to his ale. No bubbles in his palver. Hackneyed facts and shoddy ideas. Miraculously inept'" (1990, 133).[4] Students did not tolerate this kind of pedantic teaching style, favoring instead a more dialogic style that allowed them to participate actively in debate and discussion. As Brookwood student Mary Goff explained in a presentation to members of WEB, "'We do not feel that great barrier between instructor and the students. We ask questions freely and when we have opinions we express them. We are stimulated to ask, to find out, to dig ourselves'" (Howlett 1993, 65).

The erasure of hierarchies, emphasis on critical inquiry, and encouragement of dialogue that Goff describes were integral to language instruction at Brookwood. Rhetorical instruction took the surprisingly current and familiar forms of writing across the curriculum, collaborative learning, mixed-ability tutoring ("shared learning"), public speaking, labor journalism, and play writing. According to Goff, students' writing experiences at Brookwood taught them not only to write "correctly" but to see and take advantage of the connections between writing and thinking: She explained that "her English class not only taught her 'how to formulate sentences correctly and to write compositions' but also to attack 'problems and [get] down to the bottom immediately'" (Howlett 1993, 65). Another indication of Brookwood's progressive writing pedagogies is the value the school placed on workers' own language. As Susan Kates points out, "pedagogical approaches [at Brookwood] celebrated linguistic differences" and "students, though instructed in 'standard' English, were urged to use the workingman's vernacular to attract other laborers to the union cause" (1995, 122). These glimpses into Brookwood's classroom practices suggest that at Brookwood writing instruction moved beyond the teaching of basic skills associated with functional literacy and that faculty conceived of literacy as a social construct.

Like writing instruction in English classes, composition assignments across the curriculum were designed to do more than just allow faculty to correct students' surface errors and deviations from "standard" English. In Brookwood's antiwar summer school, writing was required in all classes, usually to augment class discussion. Typical assignments "generated introspective as well as expository analysis" (Howlett 1993, 186). In two- to three-page essays, students were asked to respond to provocative questions such as "Would you support a defensive war fought by the U.S.? A war fought for colonial independence? A war against a fascist state? A war in which the U.S. was the ally of the Soviet Union?" (Howlett 1993, 186–87). Charles F. Howlett, author of a 1993 history of Brookwood, writes that students' arguments, which began on paper, often spilled over into heated debates outside the classroom (1993, 187). Through such provocative writing assignments, faculty sought to spark debate and discussion, eschewing traditional lecture methods of instruction in favor of cooperative learning.

Since Brookwood faculty valued what students could teach one another, especially when they brought mixed writing abilities and educational backgrounds to the classroom, cooperative learning naturally became the pedagogy of choice. Some students came to Brookwood with only a grade school education, others struggled with English as second language, and others lacked formal education but brought a strong background in labor history and union politics. To create shared-learning environments, faculty designed innovative assignments that relied heavily on writing, research, and social construction of knowledge. One such course—taught by Brookwood's most radical teacher, Arthur Calhoun, a sociology instructor—is recalled by Carolyn Heist, a member of the Garment Workers Union. Heist explained how Calhoun would begin with his "usual diatribe against capitalism and then [divide] us into research committees with good readers distributed among the committees." Working together, students learned how to discuss, organize, communicate, and defend the findings of their research (Howlett 1993, 66).

This spirit of cooperation carried over into the labor journalism courses as students collaborated to produce the *Brookwood Review* (1923–1934), a newspaper that published editorials and articles by students and faculty on issues ranging from social activities to educational theories to commentary on current issues. Articles in the *Review* and other student publications often drew upon students' previous work experience and their involvement in labor unions (Howlett 1993, 360). Similarly, in composition courses, students' personal experiences became the starting point for broader social and cultural analysis and critique. Students who attended Brookwood during the Depression documented their experiences in case histories with titles such as "My Experience of Being Unemployed," "What Made Me Hold On," and "Searching for Bread" (Howlett 1993, 64).

The experiences students chronicled in writing classes often became the material for plays students wrote and produced on campus. Originally, the dramas mainly served entertainment purposes. But the dramas increasingly focused on social issues, especially the working conditions and labor disputes of urban textile and garment workers. Since many of the workers from these urban factories were Russian Jewish immigrants, the dramas often reflected their strong Socialist sympathies along with the faculty's growing dissatisfaction with the American Federation of Labor.[5] In Brookwood's later years, the socialist bent of these dramatic presentations became a highly visible sign of the school's political shift away from the more conservative views of the AFL, a shift that ultimately led to a loss of funding and contributed to the closing of the college.

Bryn Mawr Summer School for Women Workers

Whereas Brookwood was created through collaborative efforts between trade union leaders, socialists, and left intellectuals, the Bryn Mawr Summer School for Women Workers was a university-sponsored program whose founder, Bryn Mawr College President M. Carey Thomas, had a more feminist than Marxist agenda. In 1921, led by director Hilda Worthington Smith, Bryn Mawr's first summer school brought together privileged Bryn Mawr students, middle-class faculty, and working-class women students. Thomas, a suffragist and feminist educator, developed the school for women workers on the assumption that education would lead to women's individual self-improvement. Because she believed that an effective democratic society depended upon an educated citizenry, her vision of the school's mission had more in common with the individualistic focus of early lyceums than with the collectivist goals of Brookwood. However, a close look at the school's curriculum, faculty, and graduates reveals the leftist influences on the program in general and on writing instruction in particular.

In her 1994 study of autobiographical writing at Bryn Mawr, Karyn Hollis identifies these influences on faculty's pedagogy: "worker education and adult education movements in the United States and abroad, Dewyan educational philosophy, leftist and liberal thought, and to a certain extent, feminist principles" (34). Bryn Mawr students took courses in economics, political science, labor studies, composition, and literature. By 1926, these courses were arranged in interdisciplinary groups, with composition and literature paired with economics, **political** science, and labor studies. Groups of twenty women took all their classes together, which must have given the women a sense of confidence and solidarity. Building the women's confidence was essential for the faculty's nonhierarchical teaching methods to succeed. As at Brookwood, the faculty at Bryn Mawr encouraged active student participation in the classroom and in curriculum development, always using students' personal experiences as the starting point for discussion and debate (Hollis 1994, 34). Although at Bryn Mawr labor union issues did not dominate the curriculum as they did at Brookwood, the underlying goal of the courses was to teach students to understand their place in the larger economic system and through that understanding find ways to transform oppressive conditions in their own lives.

Bryn Mawr's approach to teaching writing—like Brookwood's progressive pedagogies—incorporated techniques we consider modern, such as collaborative learning, drafting and revision, "assignments which link personal experience with work or academic disciplines, student publications, . . . and [Freirean 'problem-posing'] assignments which encourage students to see aspects of their experience as problems which can be resolved" (Hollis 1994, 35). As Hollis points out, personal experience became the cornerstone for writing instruction with every Summer School composition class, beginning with the teacher assigning an autobiography. These autobiographies provided the faculty with a better understanding of their students' personal and work experiences, a vehicle for discussing the issue of socioeconomic class, and an invaluable tool for planning relevant lesson plans. For the Summer School students, the autobiographies became a means for writing their experiences into the curriculum and for educating the more privileged faculty about the struggles of working-class women. The autobiographies represented a site of shared learning not only between students but between faculty and students (1994, 36).

To demonstrate how the autobiography assignment encouraged students "to take a critical perspective on their lives," Hollis shows how Ellen Kennan, who taught at the school for thirteen years, revised the assignment over the years to include questions that invited critique of bourgeois values: "What beliefs and ideas that you have grown up in [sic] are you beginning to question? What ones have you cast aside entirely? What first caused you to question accepted ideas? Do you now challenge some things that you formerly considered sacred?" (1994, 38). The autobiographies not only gave students a sense of self but perhaps more importantly, as Hollis suggests, seemed to provide them with a starting point for thinking about how family values and institutions such as the church and school had helped to shape their identities and their actions (1994, 39).

Many of the autobiographies from the various English classes were published in the *Shop and School,* the student magazine. Hollis lists the various titles of the narratives and explains how they fell into three main categories: work narratives, education narratives, and utopian narratives. As the Depression took hold of the country and labor struggles increased, the titles of the work narratives reflected the changing times. Earlier titles such as "Waste in My Shop" and "A Working Girl Speaks" were replaced by titles that revealed the difficulty in finding work and the women's involvement in labor disputes: "A Day Searching for a Job," "My First Arrest," and "The 1931 Hosiery Strike." The importance of documenting and publishing the women's experiences is reinforced in comments by Esther Peterson, who began teaching at the Summer School in 1930: "I'll never forget sitting down with Jane [Smith] and having her explain that what we needed to do was to have the students see the whole world and where they fit into it. We didn't have textbooks. . . . The program was built out of their lives, and it began with who they were and where they were" (1996, 64).

While the women's personal and work histories provided the foundation for the school's curriculum, the students' course work and extracurricular activities often helped them envision ways to expand their realms of influence and experience. As Peterson explains,

> the program was a training ground for women to develop leadership. We had mock meetings, for example. They said they would never dare to stand up at union meetings in front of all the men. But we helped them and taught them how. We put on plays. We now call it role playing. They'd take parts. They took the parts of the boss, the workers, the citizens. The whole point was to be practical . . . where you are now, not some theoretical event down the pike. (1996, 63)

The Summer School took the idea of making an impact "where you are now" literally by creating for students avenues through which they could participate in democratic decision making from the moment they arrived at Bryn Mawr. Director Hilda Smith insisted on a "tremendously strong democratic process . . . the faculty having a say and the students having a say" (Peterson 1996, 63). As a result of this democratic experience, many students testify to the transformative effects of the Summer School program. Carmen Lucia's contribution to *Rocking the Boat,* an oral history of union women, is a case in point. A student in the eight-week program of 1927, Lucia, a garment worker who went on to become an organizer for the United Hatters, Cap and Millinery

Workers International Union, describes her Bryn Mawr experience in glowing terms: "My world kept getting bigger and bigger, and I was getting more and more excited. I was having skates on my feet and wings on my body. I wanted to fly where I heard of anything that was worthwhile" (1996, 41).

Lucia's testimony is representative of numerous Bryn Mawr graduates who went on to play leadership roles in trade unions and workers education in their own communities. Ironically, the feeling of empowerment that Lucia and other Summer School graduates felt as result of activist pedagogies ultimately led to the demise of the school itself. Although historians such as Altenbaugh characterize the Summer School's mission as "apolitical" (1990, 48), in reality it was the increasingly overt politicization of the faculty and students that contributed to the Bryn Mawr Board of Directors cutting the school's funding and forcing it to move in 1935 to an off-campus location.

In the late 1930s and early 1940s, as the political climate in the United States became less sympathetic to socialist ideas, the impetus for workers education shifted away from social and political activism. As a result, education for working people began returning to its meritocratic roots. But even though the ideology of self-improvement associated with the mechanics institutes and lyceums regained dominance in the 1940s and 1950s, the politicized curricula and radical pedagogies of the labor colleges leave a legacy for today's writing teachers, especially for educators of working adults interested in Freirean critical pedagogies. As this chapter has shown, the student-centered, dialogic pedagogies practiced in the labor colleges resemble the Freirean method of literacy education. Since Freire himself has cautioned against applying his critical pedagogy in the U.S. context, where issues of socioeconomic class often remain invisible, writing instruction in labor colleges provides an important historical model for critical literacy education in the United States.

Notes

1. For a more detailed discussion of the lyceum movement, see Carl Bode (1956), *The American Lyceum: Town Meeting of the Mind*.

2. Historians such as Altenbaugh and Sinclair do not specify to what extent these unskilled workers participated in lyceums and mechanics institutes, although Sinclair does point out that the mechanics institutes were typical of "educational reforms initially designed to benefit poor and disadvantaged artisans" that "usually served a more literate clientele" (Sinclair 1974, ix).

3. Details about writing pedagogies and assignments for a variety of courses are available through Brookwood's archives, through the work of historians

such as Richard J. Altenbaugh and Marius Hansome (who taught course at Brookwood), and, most recently, through Susan Kates' 1995 dissertation. Kates' work makes an important contribution to the history of writing instruction by tracing the roots of critical pedagogies in the United States to the activist education of labor colleges such as Brookwood. She points out that educational theorists such as Henry Giroux often attribute the origins of critical pedagogy in the United States to Paulo Freire and the radical ideas of the 1960s. As Kates argues, looking more closely at the pedagogies of Brookwood College may provide an even more useful model for literacy instruction in the United States than Freire's work in Brazil.

4. Not only could students dismiss faculty, but faculty could also dismiss students who did not keep up with assignments.

5. As Altenbaugh and other historians have noted, Brookwood students and faculty became increasingly critical of many AFL leaders and policies. Altenbaugh explains that "by the end of the decade, Brookwood had become an irritant to AFL leaders through its classroom training and labor activism [and] its institutes." In various labor publications, students and faculty accused the AFL of being "coopted by bourgeois society" (1990, 179).

Chapter Two

From Vocationalism to Liberal Arts Education

Writing Instruction in Unions, Universities, and Community Colleges, 1935–1970

The decisions of the future are too important to be left to a very small elite. All of us must learn to know the problems that affect our homes, our communities, our jobs, and our world, and attempt to find the wisdom to resolve them. Liberal education for workers can help.

—Emery F. Bacon, director of
the Department of Education
of the United Steelworkers of
America, *Orientation in Labor
Education: A Symposium on
Liberal Education for Labor in
the University*

In the late 1930s, as the well-known workers education programs associated with the labor colleges lost funding, the most viable workers education programs became those with strong union ties. New unions for automobile, steel, and rubber workers developed workers education programs, but the emphasis had shifted from a broadly philosophical socialist agenda to a more narrowly "utilitarian [focus concerned with] sustaining the trade union movement; leadership training and the need for membership loyalty became paramount." Courses lost the critical edge that characterized instruction in earlier programs including those at Brookwood and Bryn Mawr (Altenbaugh 1990, 45).

The utilitarian education that characterized union-sponsored workers education programs in the late 1930s marked the beginning of the growing trend of vocationalism that would shape curriculum of education for workers in the 1940s and 1950s. This trend toward vocationalism in union education programs meant that the onus for literacy instruction for working adults fell to writing faculty in the growing number of two-year colleges, where many working-class students, including working adults, found themselves in vocational programs. These two-year college programs emphasized utilitarian goals that would prepare worker-students for jobs rather than teaching them critical literacy or providing the kind of liberal arts education advocated by progressive educators like Dewey. By the late fifties, the trend toward vocationalism was disrupted as unions and universities began working cooperatively to develop liberal arts-based programs for workers.

These mid-twentieth century trends in the history of education for working adults—first toward vocationalism, then toward liberal arts-based curricula—can be seen as reconfigurations of the two educational goals for working adults we identified in the nineteenth and early twentieth centuries: self-improvement and upward mobility in the mechanics institutes and class consciousness in the labor colleges. Just as vocationalism reflects the values of self-improvement, liberal arts-based education reflects the labor colleges' emphasis on giving workers skills in critical analysis through broad exposure to philosophical ideas. These trends in the way educators frame their goals for workers education reflect an ongoing cycle that still shapes writing instruction for working adults.

Vocationalism in the American Federation of Labor

The onset of World War II led to a national tacit agreement that it would be unpatriotic to engage in labor conflicts at a time when production of industrial products was essential to the success of the war effort. Skills training that might lead to increased production and efficiency took precedence over any remnants of the radical, philosophical education of the 1920s and 1930s. Evidence of the increasingly conservative shift of the AFL's approach to workers education abounds in its 1953 *Reports of the Executive Council and the Annual Convention of the American Federation of Labor on Education*. The language of the report emphasizes preserving the status quo, suggesting that education should "help preserve moral and social values" and "preserve our civilization" (AFL 1954, 11).[1]

The AFL report stresses that the goal of workers education is to produce good workers, not necessarily effective critical thinkers. Philosophically, the AFL-sponsored programs sought to prepare workers to adapt to demands of an increasingly mechanized workplace, not to reflect upon the larger political and economic implications of workplace changes. Because these programs defined their goals in narrowly vocational terms, their directors may not have seen any need for literacy beyond basic reading and writing skills, and we found no evidence that writing instruction played a role in vocation training offered through the AFL.

Vocationalism in the Two-Year Colleges

While community-based vocational educational programs and increasingly conservative unions remained avenues for workers education throughout the 1950s, a growing number of workers turned to the rapidly expanding two-year colleges for education. These worker-students found themselves in institutions frought with conflicting notions of their educational aims for working-class people. The number of community and junior colleges grew steadily throughout the 1920s and 1930s, with explosive growth occurring in the 1960s. The new two-year college students consisted of working-class and minority veterans on the GI Bill, along with growing numbers of adults taking evening classes while working full or part time (Raines 1993, 101). Working students found these close-to-home colleges, many of which began as high school extensions, convenient to attend even while working shifts and taking care of family responsibilities (Shor 1987a, 15). By the late sixties, the student population at two-year colleges was predominantly working class: Forty-five percent of the students came from "upper blue collar families," 17 percent were unskilled workers, 23 percent held white-collar jobs, and "the remainder [were] from proprietary, managerial, professional backgrounds" (Wisgoski 1971, 185–86). During 1960 and 1961, there were 663 two-year colleges in the United States, with 510,000 traditional students and 206,000 adult education students (Cross 1961, 131–33).

Reasons for the two-year colleges' exponential growth in the 1960s and assessments of the quality of education they provided working-class people differ depending on the critical perspective used to examine the two-year college movement. Critics point out that while these institutions offered students convenient locations, open admission, and affordable tuition, they often participated in a "cooling-out" process. That is, colleges use the dream of a four-year degree to attract students;

once they enroll, rather than encouraging them to prepare for transfer to a four-year institution, the schools track them into vocational programs. Educational critics have attributed this "cooling out" to factors ranging from "sophisticated thought control" to community colleges' inability "to reconcile many different and often antithetical goals" (Shor 1987a, 17–18; Dougherty 1994, 106).

Of course, some working adults actively sought out the vocational programs and never intended to pursue four-year degrees.[2] But no matter why or how working-class adults found themselves in two-year college vocational programs, questions about the quality and ethics of the programs remain. Unlike the workers attending the labor colleges and other workers education programs of the past, worker-students sought two- or four-year college credentials to compete in a job market where the number of desirable jobs was limited and where employers increasingly favored people with at least some higher education. Unfortunately, when the two-year colleges misjudged the demand for various vocational skills, worker-students' investments in higher education did not pay off as they expected. This tendency to "overshoot" and "undershoot" the labor market's demands leads critics such as Ira Shor to describe the two-year college as a "warehouse" where "surplus labor is stored" (Dougherty 1994, 44–46; Shor 1987a, 6). However, even amid his harsh criticism, Shor acknowledges the contradictory nature of the two-year colleges, calling them "ironic gifts from the state." As Shor writes, even with their vocational emphasis, the colleges "[opened] up critical spaces not available in other spheres," and with the advent of women's and civil rights movements, real possibilities existed for critical dialogue, even if only in single classrooms (Shor 1987a, 22). Shor's mixed review of the two-year college creates a picture of these schools as sites where democratic education might occasionally emerge but was unlikely to flourish.

Writing Instruction in the Two-Year Colleges. A close examination of the curricula of two-year colleges during the 1960s reflects the contradictory pedagogies and educational ideologies that worker-students would have encountered in all their classes, including writing courses. Throughout the decade, faculty and administrators debated the proper place of general education courses in the two-year college curriculum as well as the quality of vocational education programs. Most participants in the debate agree that the two-year colleges frequently made two kinds of curricular mistakes: On one hand, they imposed elitist ideas of liberal education and traditional "banking" models of instruction on their working-class transfer students; on the other hand, they scaled down curriculum to offer vocational students "no frills" education with much of the intellectual rigor removed.

Vocational programs' narrow emphasis on job skills frequently neglected critical and scientific inquiry, widening the gap between the working class and liberally educated middle- and upper-class people. Because vocational programs usually lack a critical edge, sociologist Fred Pincus argues that they mislead students and become a "way of adjusting [working-class and minority] students' aspirations to present economic realities." He sees a potential for effective vocational education, but only if programs provide students "with a historical and political context from which to understand the dismal choices they face." With such a context, "vocational education students might then begin to raise some fundamental questions about the legitimacy of educational, political, and economic institutions in the United States" (Pincus 1986, 226). The liberatory pedagogy that Pincus calls for represents the democratic ideals that inspired the creation of two-year colleges but that rarely filtered down to classroom practices. For the most part, two-year colleges missed a unique opportunity to provide alternative and innovative education for the working-class people they served.

One of the relatively few educators who recognized the exciting potential of the two-year college as a new kind of educational experiment was Roger Garrison, chair of the Department of Language and Literature at Westbrook Junior College during the 1960s. In a presentation to the New England Junior College Council, Garrison offered a sharp critique of two-year colleges' liberal arts pedagogy, arguing that courses in literature, the fine arts, social history, and the sciences were too often taught to "reward memory, rote, easy generalization, and intellectual dependence on textbook and instructor" (1971, 232–33). Minute by minute, he details his observations of the "best" teachers' courses, in which students rarely spoke while teachers lectured on snippets of literary and political history and devoured class time taking attendance. Based on interviews with thousands of two-year college faculty, Garrison shows how uncertain faculty felt about the aims of the two-year colleges. One faculty member he spoke with complained that "when you poke into the business of 'aims,' you get fog, jargon, catalog talk about the open door and 'service to students.'" As a result, that teacher decided simply to focus on basic skills instruction—"how to write a clear sentence or how to read a paragraph and understand what it means" (Garrison 1971, 234).

For Garrison, the ideal aim of liberal arts education in the two-year college clearly should be more ambitious; the goal should be to help make students feel *effectively at home*, both in this pluralistic technological society and in the multi-cultured society of this tiny planet of warring neighborhoods." An admirer of education theorist Alfred North Whitehead, Garrison argued for active learning and praised vocational instructors who, like one teacher he interviewed, went beyond teaching metalworking skills to introduce students to metallurgy—the history of metals—some physics and chemistry, and even issues of union membership (1971, 236–39). However, because so few teachers saw the potential for combining active learning, general education, and vocational or liberal arts instruction, education in the two-year colleges rigidified into a two-tier system, with both tracks lacking creative, transformative pedagogies.

By the mid-1960s, the National Council of Teachers of English became concerned enough about an impending "crisis" that they sponsored a national conference at Arizona State University in Tempe on the teaching of English in the two-year college. In his keynote address at the 1965 conference, Albert Kitzhaber explained how the "explosive enrollment" gave him a sense of urgency regarding the problems of teaching English in the two-year college. He especially feared that the Vocational Education Act would lead colleges to substitute "vocational English" for "more generalized and liberal courses" (1965, 2). Along with alerting the profession to the increasing pressure to vocationalize English curricula, the Tempe conference proceedings address a wide range of problems: composition instructors facing large classes and therefore assigning little writing; English faculty lacking advanced study in linguistics, basic writing methodology, and speech; and faculty defining the aims of first-year writing courses in significantly disparate ways (Weingarten and Kroeger 1965, 4–59).

These problems existed in "regular" first-year writing courses, but they were amplified in the "remedial" and credit-bearing adult education classes. Whereas the Tempe conference proceedings express concern about the focus on "functional" grammar taught in regular courses, usually during conferences rather than in class, teachers of remedial classes reported feeding their students a steady diet of grammar exercises in class, which meant they received little practice in actual composition. In "English Courses for Adults and Community Services," an article in the conference proceedings, Aileen Creighton describes the exasperation felt by many two-year college teachers in designing English courses for working adults, a group that includes "people of quite varied abilities, ages, purposes, needs, and proficiencies [who] somehow land together in evening school English 601a." The following description shows the diversity that created what some instructors described as "an impossible and maddening teaching situation":

> A laborer who has suddenly decided to go to college because he hears that only the educated man can get ahead comes to the registration table and asks for—well, what is the one course that he can be sure is absolutely required? English 601a, of course. A young salesman seeks a course to teach him "grammar" so that he can be, presumably,

> more persuasive: what else but 601a? A petroleum engineer with a
> fresh B.S., helpless before the report writing his job demands, re-
> members freshman English: why not take it again? An exquisitely ed-
> ucated medical doctor from Argentina, in residence for a year at a lo-
> cal hospital, wants a course to polish his conversational English: what
> more plausible than something described as the "beginning course"?
> (1965, 85)

The result of many writing teachers' attempts to design courses to meet
these adult students' varying needs resulted in disappointed students
and high attrition rates.

Creighton's essay laments the gap between the needs of a diverse
student body and an English curriculum developed for a prototypical
college student—a well-prepared, middle-class high school graduate.
Her analysis of the state of writing instruction for working adults reveals that students who didn't fit the prototype were often perceived by
even the most enlightened educators as the "can't learns and won't
learns and don't learns." In fairness, Creighton does emphasize the importance of placing "the most dismal, ill-prepared, and unable students" in remedial English classes that focus on writing process and
"matters of content, thought, reasoning," eschewing the standard fare
of remedial instruction (1965, 86). Her recommendations for designing
effective remedial English classes anticipate some of the teaching strategies described in Mina Shaughnessy's 1975 *Errors and Expectations*. However, in the interim between Creighton's 1965 essay and Shaughnessy's
groundbreaking book, it is not hard to imagine inappropriate curricula
in courses like English 601a contributing to the washing out or cooling
out of working adult students.

Despite the high attrition rate for working adults in first-year composition courses, publications in *College English, Junior College Journal, The
Educational Record,* and *The Journal of Higher Education* during the 1950s
and early 1960s reveal seemingly isolated examples of progressive, imaginative pedagogy. In "Freshman English Experiment: General Education
in a Traditional Curriculum," Paul D. Bauder calls for integration of writing across the curriculum in the two-year college (1952, 337–39). Other
articles emphasize student-centered classrooms, where students develop their own reading lists, write about home and family relationships, and create their own stories that become texts for the class.[3] Several articles even discuss strategies for reshaping the entire first-year
curriculum to make English an integral part of a liberal studies program
rather than a separate discipline focusing on isolated skills.[4]

Although these examples of progressive writing pedagogy in two-
year colleges of the 1950s are the exception rather than the rule, they
dovetail with nascent social theories of writing instruction that were
gaining influence in American colleges between 1945 and the 1960s.[5]

Importantly, as progressive educators gained influence in universities, less conservative union leaders began to question the utilitarian vision of workers education that dominated the AFL during the 1950s. These shifts to the left in universities and unions during the 1960s led university faculty and union leaders to forge coalitions that resulted in more broadly based educational programs in which liberal arts-based writing instruction played an important role.

Liberal Arts Education in Union-University Programs

With the turbulent social and political upheavals of the 1960s, union-based workers education programs participated in the spirit of inquiry that inspired curricular change in institutions of higher education throughout the country. During this time, composition studies became an increasingly pluralistic discipline: Many writing instructors continued to apply the arhetorical approaches to composition that formed the foundation of most vocational tracks at two-year colleges in the 1950s; others began developing new pedagogies to meet students' demands for curricula relevant to pressing issues of racism, sexism, war, and peace. As Berlin points out, a 1968 issue of *College Composition and Communication* included pieces on approaches to teaching writing to the culturally diverse students who were entering college in ever-increasing numbers (1987, 140). The authors of these articles found a receptive audience among liberal educators, who had begun to identify cultural biases in the traditional liberal arts curriculum, which relied heavily on canonical authors and standardized tests with built-in middle-class assumptions about cultural literacy (Aronowitz and Giroux 1985, 2).

Even as traditional liberal arts programs faced critique at four-year colleges, leaders in workers education began to see the value of liberal arts education for working adults. Beginning in the early 1960s, labor educators argued that programs for workers needed to move beyond the utilitarian concerns of the 1940s and 1950s to include liberal arts education. To provide a less skills-focused curricula for workers, unions sought to take advantage of the resources available through two-year colleges and universities.

At a 1963 symposium sponsored by the National Institute of Labor Education titled "Challenges to Labor Education in the 60s," academicians became involved in discussions over the future of workers education. In one article from the symposium proceedings, New York State School of Industrial Relations Professor Ralph Campbell points out the lack of adult educational opportunities for blue- and white-collar workers alike, even in large cities. He calls for universities and two-year colleges to "take a more positive role in the development of programs which bring together [leaders in labor, management, and adult education] to discuss major problems of our society in the relaxed atmosphere of educational seminars" (1962, 64). For leaders to effectively participate in this kind of problem solving, Campbell suggests the need for labor education that combines academic study with individualized mentoring programs designed to give prospective union leaders insight into the broader perspectives of already successful leaders. He writes favorably of experiments with workers studying humanities and the arts as one means of fostering labor leaders' professional growth (1962, 66). Campbell's article is important because it signals a shift away from the skill-based programs of unions and two-year colleges in the 1940s and 1950s. His work also supports the experimental move made to meld labor education with liberal education that was already going on in a few innovative programs.

The country's most innovative labor education programs of the 1960s are discussed in the proceedings from the 1962 "Reorientation in Labor Education" symposium sponsored by the Center for the Study of Liberal Education for Adults. Like Campbell's article, this symposium focused on moving labor education "beyond the narrow utilitarian ends of the traditional bargaining and management courses that still comprise[d] the bulk of labor education in this country" (Goldman 1962, 1). The participants in the symposium sought to define what a liberal education for labor would mean and how unions and universities would work together to design effective curricula and teaching methods for working adults. For most participants, the essence of a "liberal" education constituted "education for the rights and responsibilities of freedom, personal and social," through the "continuing development of each individual" for the purpose of creating an "increasingly democratic society" (Kornbluh 1962, 89). Since most unions could not independently finance long-term education for their members, the question became how universities could provide these key ingredients of a liberal education through courses attractive to unions and working people.

The need to infuse labor education with a more liberal course of study evolved from union leaders' and labor educators' belief that unions' influence in society was growing and that growth called for "leadership broadly educated" (Goldman 1962, 1). These union leaders and educators also reasoned that with leisure time on the rise, men and women would need an education in the arts and sciences to fully utilize their free time and contribute positively to society. They argued that workers, like their more elite counterparts, had the right to an "education not designed for any extrinsic end, but to bring about results 'somehow terminating in and intrinsic to the one being educated'"

(Goldman 1962, 2). In the five union-university education programs featured at the 1962 symposium, this somewhat abstract goal of education for education's sake—along liberal education's emphasis on analysis and self-reflection—underpinned the choices each program's directors made regarding teaching methodologies, curricula, and instructors. The five featured programs all began between 1957 and 1961, with each program giving worker-students "bread and butter" courses on unionism seasoned to varying degrees with courses in the arts and sciences.

University of California Liberal Arts for Labor Program

From its inception, the University of California Liberal Arts for Labor Program debated to what extent courses in social sciences and the humanities could replace the "practical" tool courses in unionism. Working with their Labor Planning Committee, program director Anne Gould successfully made social science courses the foundation of the curriculum with only occasional humanities offerings. One experimental course, Contemporary Ideas, included readings by Galbraith (*Affluent Society*), Fromm (*Sane Society*), Lubell (*Future of American Politics*), and Bronowski (*Science and Human Values*). These readings sparked lively discussions that encouraged students to analyze and debate abstract ideas. This course and others like it relied on a lecture-discussion format that required a flexible instructor that fit the program's profile of the ideal instructor: willing to experiment with methods and materials and bringing "an interest in the students as people, and a general sympathy for the goals of labors," though not necessarily "an outright prolabor attitude" (Gould 1962, 34–38). Having flexible teachers was vital because of high absenteeism due to students' rotating shifts and the heterogeneous makeup of the classes in terms of educational background (some students had previously attended college; others had sixth-grade educations). The diverse educational backgrounds of students and their demanding work schedules would have made out-of-class writing assignments difficult. Based on Gould's description of teaching methods and course content, reading and class discussion rather than written work dominated the courses.

Institute Labor Program at Rutgers University

Along with reading and vigorous discussion, writing played a significant role in the liberal arts courses offered to union members through the Institute Labor Program at Rutgers University. To qualify for a noncredit trade union certificate, students had to complete twelve credit

hours in oral and written communication (out of a total of thirty credits) during two years. In addition to certificate programs, Rutgers offered a three-year institute, a program initiated in 1950 in cooperation
with the United Steelworkers of America. To liberalize the content of
third-year courses in their summer institute, Rutgers emphasized "the
whole spectrum of written communication as it applies to the problems
and challenges of leadership." Readings for the third-year courses included cross-disciplinary works ranging from the literary collection *Im-
mortal Poems of the English Language*, to the anthropological *Patterns of
Culture* by Ruth Benedict, to *Good Reading*, a text offering college-level
reading strategies (Kerrison 1962, 55). By infusing the traditional labor
studies curriculum with these kinds of cross-disciplinary readings and
requiring additional practice in writing, the Rutgers program consciously chose to provide workers with a broad-based liberal education
that addressed the needs of "the whole man" (Kerrison 1962, 60).

Resident Study Program for Union Staff (University of California at Berkeley, Cornell University, and Michigan State University)

The "whole man" idea had less appeal to organizers of the Resident
Study Program for Union Staff, sponsored by the National Institute of
Labor Education and three major universities—University of California
at Berkeley, Cornell University, and Michigan State. This program was
designed to help unions maintain and increase their socioeconomic
influence by helping union leaders develop strategies for analyzing and
responding to "unprecedented problems arising from rapid social and
economic change both at home and abroad" (Allen 1962, 62). While
the program focused on study of the social sciences and humanities,
every course filtered its subject matter through the lens of unionism.
The program was less concerned with educating individuals for their
own self-actualization than with developing effective union leaders.
Most class time focused on social sciences such as economics, political
science, sociology, and psychology, with only the Berkeley program including ten units of writing out of 122 (Allen 1962, 66). Humanities
courses such as Art and Society and the American Novel, offered only
at Michigan State, were clearly the exception rather than the rule. In
describing the Resident Study Program in general, Russell Allen men-
tions little about how writing was used in any part of the program, but
he notes that to qualify for the program applicants submitted an essay
as part of their application. His statement that "ability to handle reading and writing was an obvious prerequisite" for the program suggests
that written composition was integral to the program but not a direct
focus of instruction (1962, 64).

University of Chicago Union Leadership Program

Like the Resident Study Program, the University of Chicago Union Leadership Program focused on preparing union leaders, but it subscribed to a more liberal approach to leadership education. This nonresidential program evolved from tool-focused courses in the late 1940s to a broader mission of "examining the unionist as an individual in a free society" (McCollum 1962, 77). Program developers believed in a kind of "trickle-down" theory of education: by educating union leaders, the leaders in turn could share their new perspectives with union members, and this process would contribute to building a more democratic society. The ultimate goal of the program was liberal education for action—"to provide an understanding of the over-all drift of American society: where it is going and alternative courses of action that are available" (McCollum 1962, 79). Not coincidentally for an action-oriented program, this program emphasized discussion over lecture and asked students to give voice to their ideas orally and in writing. Courses in study skills aimed to hone students' critical reading and writing abilities by focusing on "reading comprehension, notetaking, logic, and writing" (McCollum 1962, 82). To assess students' progress, end-of-course essay exams prompted students to synthesize course work through writing responses to prompts such as the following:

> There are two general ways of explaining how people get their attitudes, opinions, beliefs and behavior patterns. One explanation is that these things come from a person's personal thinking and assessment of situations. The other is that they come from the relevant groups to which people belong. What do these theories tell us about membership identification with the union? (McCollum 1962, 84)

This writing assignment reflects the program's commitment to helping worker-students analyze their personal experiences, often within unions, so that they could better understand and apply broad theories of human behavior.

United Steelworkers Fourth Year Institute (Pennsylvania State University)

A similar philosophy—the belief that labor education ought to foster a love of reading and writing and inspire workers to wrestle with large, philosophical ideas—was the impetus for the creation of the United Steelworkers Fourth Year Institute titled "A World of Ideas." Originating at Penn State University, this institute capped off three years of two-week-long seminars and at one point was offered by as many as twenty-five universities. Emery F. Bacon, director of the Department of Education of the United Steelworkers of America, argues eloquently that a liberal education has too often been preserved for a privileged elite and as a result society lacks "the ideas, the men, and the conviction to solve national and international problems" (1962, 44). He points out that "education played a major role in organizing the Steelworkers Union during the 30s. It stressed the Union's responsibility to society: to dignify the individual, and to accelerate social progress" (1962, 45). This commitment to education led the union to create the initial institute in 1946.

Like the programs discussed above, the institute began with a practical focus, offering union tool courses (i.e., collective bargaining and labor organizing). Eventually, a second-year program focused on "citizenship responsibility," then a third year was added to address "leadership," and finally a controversial Fourth Year Institute on the liberal arts became available at certain universities (some considered its liberal arts focus "frivolous"). The goals of the Steelworkers Fourth Year Institute resound with the "educating the whole man" philosophy that was present in most of the union-university labor education programs of the 1960s, although a distinguishing feature of the Steelworkers Fourth Year Institute was its emphasis on developing creativity. Unfortunately, in describing the institute, Bacon gives little detail about how instructors used writing and literature to achieve the goals of the program.

The push for liberal education for working people that took place in these five programs by no means represented a significant national trend to educate workers. Even so, these programs are important in the history of workers education and in educational history in general, because they attempted to democratize education. The union-university programs, as they sought ways to make the liberal arts relevant to working people, created innovative curricula that gave equal value to the voices of revered writers and thinkers and the experiences of worker-students. By coalescing liberal arts education with union tool courses and working-class experience, union-university programs of the 1960s anticipated the formation in the 1970s of separate adult-oriented colleges where working people could pursue either professional or liberal arts degrees.

Notes

1. To ensure that the curriculum remained overtly apolitical, the report supports the state's right to "[prohibit] against the employment of Communists as teachers," arguing that "a Communist is subject to party control; a good teacher must be free" (AFL 1954, 11). This statement demonstrates how thor-

oughly the postwar McCarthyism reinforced the AFL's desire to separate itself from the radical education that was the foundation of the labor colleges.

2. Dougherty points out that at the two-year college, enrollments in vocational education "rose from 20 percent of all community college students in fall 1959 to 29 percent in fall 1968 and to 40 to 60 percent in the mid-1980s." Students "receiving vocational degrees and certifications rose from 49 percent in 1970–1971 to 65 percent in 1978–1979" (1994, 192–93).

3. See E. L. Brown, "Teaching Sophomore Literature: Conference Method," *College English* 16 (1955): 296–302; George Robert Carlson, "The Contributions of English to Home and Family Living," *Junior College Journal* 20 (1949): 209–17; and M. L. McChesney, "Stimulating Enthusiasm for Creative Writing," *Junior College Journal* 27 (1956): 48–49.

4. See G. W. Gregory, "Approach to Functional English in a Four-Year Junior College," *Junior College Journal* 29 (1958): 203–5, and Anne Prisleau Jones, "Freshman Studies: An Experimental Course at Lawrence College," *The Educational Record* 35 (1954): 208–20.

5. For a detailed discussion of how social theories of writing instruction gained influence between 1945 and 1960, see James A. Berlin (1987), *Rhetoric and Reality: Writing Instruction in American Colleges: 1900–1985*, 92–119.

Chapter Three

Teaching Critical Analysis Through the Liberal Arts at Alfred North Whitehead College

A technical or technological education, which is to have any chance of satisfying the practical needs of the nation, must be conceived in a liberal spirit as a real intellectual enlightenment in regard to principles applied and services rendered. In such an education geometry and poetry are as essential as turning laths.

—Alfred North Whitehead,
*The Aims of Education and
Other Essays*

In the 1970s, a small liberal arts college, the University of Redlands, joined the larger public universities that had become involved in educating working adults through liberal arts-based programs. In 1971, the University of Redlands, in Redlands, California, began offering college-credit courses for working adults through its new Special Programs Office. The early program attracted students employed in professional settings, along with many hoping to leave behind blue- or pink-collar positions through education. In 1976, the Alfred North Whitehead Col-

28

lege was established. Today, Whitehead College serves approximately 2,200 adults, with the "average" student being thirty-six years old and working as a midlevel manager (Fraiberg 1997, 1). The college offers a blend of liberal arts and professional training that reflects its liaisons with business and its affiliation with a respected liberal arts college, the University of Redlands. Whitehead College's mission statement emphasizes a commitment to developing relevant, flexible programs for adults that "unite imaginative skills of liberal studies, with the practical elements central to their occupations" (Robertson 1997, 11).

In March of 1997, we visited Whitehead's main campus in Redlands, interviewing program directors, deans, and faculty. Through these conversations, we learned the history of their programs, how they are administered, and the nature of writing instruction students receive. Faculty and administrators explained how most Whitehead College students progress through their programs in clusters, with groups of students moving together through a lock-step series of courses as they pursue undergraduate degrees in Liberal Studies, Business and Management, or Information Systems. The college also offers three masters degree programs in Business Administration, Management, and Education. The people we spoke with generously shared details about the college's experiential learning courses and a new course in Advanced Writing and Critical Analysis required for Business and Management majors.

We identify three strong influences on writing instruction at Whitehead: Redland's commitment to liberal arts-based education, businesses' request for relevant work-related curriculum, and working students' desire for pedagogies and instructional delivery modes that meet their unique needs. These factors have led to writing curricula that combine analysis of students' personal and working lives with rhetorical and cultural analysis of texts in the liberal arts tradition.

Responding to Needs of Working Adults

From its inception, one of Whitehead's greatest strengths has been its insistence upon identifying the needs of working adults and putting those needs at the center of program and curriculum development. At the same time, Whitehead's adaptations for nontraditional students— most notably, accelerated classes, credit for experiential learning, and off-campus courses—have led to an uneasy coexistence with University of Redlands. As C. Alton Robertson explained in his history of Whitehead College, many Redlands administrators and faculty over the years resisted the idea of a separate college for adult students:

> It has taken most of the two decades since the establishment of White-
> head College for the animosity created by that action and the suspi-
> cions and doubts about separate, non-traditional adult education with
> accelerated programs, the assessment of experiential learning, depen-
> dence on adjunct faculty, and a student body composed mainly of per-
> sons who did not fit the University's image of its students and alumni
> to be overcome and for Whitehead College to be seen as an integral
> unit of the University of Redlands. (Robertson 1997, 13)

Despite resistance from Redlands, in the early 1970s the adult programs
continued to grow and eventually gained status as a separate college—
the Alfred North Whitehead College of Liberal and Career Studies,
named after the distinguished mathematician and philosopher who
worked to create the Open University for working adults at University
of London.

Convenient Locations

Beginning with the first extension courses, working adults took advantage of Whitehead's degree programs in part because the college offered courses at various locations throughout Southern California. Today, the college reaches adult students through satellite "centers" in
Southern California that often redefine the traditional picture of a college classroom. Although Whitehead College's main center at University of Redlands has all the charm of a picturesque, small-town private
university, many Whitehead courses are taught in satellite facilities,
perhaps a hotel conference room or a meeting room in a corporate
headquarters, where working adult students find it convenient to attend class and meet with advisors. Four regional centers, located at
Irvine, San Diego, Burbank, and Torrance, offer students additional resources including minilibraries, lounges, permanent classrooms, com-
puters labs, academic advisors, and enrollment managers (Robertson
1997, 30). This decentralized model for delivering education makes
Whitehead a forerunner in the current rush to develop distance education programs that appeal to working adults who lack the time to
commute to university campuses.[1]

Along with serving individual adults through off-campus courses,
Whitehead also develops off-campus corporate partnership programs
and clusters of courses that are tailored in part to the needs of participating companies. Three courses in Whitehead College's corporate program offerings in the Master of Arts in Management (MAM) degree
program vary depending on the client's needs, according to an interview with Dean of Admissions Mike Kraft on March 18, 1997. The
more flexible the college can be in terms of course content, time spent
in the classroom, and location of classes, the more corporations express

interest in programs for their employees. Because companies are not always satisfied with an "off-the-shelf program," Whitehead College faculty working in the MAM program generally tailor about 20 percent of their course content to the particular needs of a corporation. For example, if a company is reorganizing, issues surrounding the process of reorganization might become a touchstone for the MAM degree courses. For corporate workers needing a complete on-site baccalaureate program, Whitehead College's Connections Program gradually initiates students with little or no college experience into a degree program by first offering remedial work in writing and mathematics.

To staff its decentralized courses, Whitehead participates in the growing controversial trend of relying on a large staff of part-time faculty, who teach all but a few of the college's courses.[2] Relying so heavily on part-time faculty allows Whitehead the financial means and the flexibility to continue expanding programs and course offerings to an ever-widening audience. While easy access to courses benefits working adults who might not otherwise enroll in classes, extensive reliance on part-time faculty challenges Whitehead to find ways of maintaining acceptable levels of quality and consistency among their satellite courses. To do so, Whitehead has developed a complex and detailed teacher certification process that is coordinated by "lead faculty" who are responsible for curriculum development and adjunct faculty hiring.[3] Because of their careful certification process, Whitehead faculty believe they avoid the most common problem encountered by institutions that rely heavily on part-time faculty—resorting to last-minute, emergency hiring and continuing employment based solely on seniority rather than classroom performance, student evaluations, and up-to-date credentials. Through its comprehensive teacher certification process, Whitehead College attempts to deliver on its promise of high-quality instruction at convenient locations.

A careful process of hiring adjunct faculty is a key to ensuring academic integrity, according to the writing program's lead faculty member, Allison Fraiberg. When a new writing course is introduced or an old one significantly revised, Fraiberg requires letters of application that outline an applicant's qualifications for teaching the new or revised course.[4] According to a March 18, 1997, interview with Fraiberg and Donna Shaeffer, the lead faculty member for Information Systems, the hiring process then continues as usual, with Fraiberg examining candidates' vitae and conducting phone interviews to determine who would be invited to the main campus for a daylong evaluation session. During that session, prospective teachers give a presentation, participate in an interview, grade a student paper, and take part in a "leaderless discussion." In these discussions, a small group of teachers gather around a table as they discuss a pedagogical issue given to them by the evaluator.

For instance, they might be asked to talk about how best to handle an incident of racism in classroom discussion. The evaluator (usually the lead teacher) observes the discussion, noting how the potential teachers handle a small-group dynamic and watching for any red flags that suggest that the teacher may not deal well with students (e.g., interrupting other people or making irrelevant comments that derail the discussion). The assessment day concludes with an orientation session in which the applicants learn about the mission of Whitehead College and what teaching in an adult environment entails (e.g., respecting the life experiences students bring to class and adapting curricula to an accelerated delivery mode). This certification process is taken extremely seriously as a means for maintaining high-quality and reasonable pedagogical consistency among courses at off-campus sites.

Accelerated Courses

Whitehead's tradition of accelerating courses has been a key to the college's success according to a March 18, 1997, interview with Lucille Sansing, then dean of Whitehead: "One thing that I think is common to all successful adult programs is the idea of acceleration. One thing that adults don't have is time. One of the things that stands in the way of adults going back to school is the prospect of working for nine years to get a degree." As Whitehead College evolved, faculty and administrators argued that all degree programs could be justifiably accelerated because they built on students' past work experience and included workplace practicum projects that gave depth to general courses in business or management (Robertson 1997, 5–10). To accelerate courses, Whitehead College reduces "seat time" (time spent in the classroom) by having fewer but longer class meetings. For instance, a typical writing course meets only six times, with each class session being taught in a four-hour block. Whitehead courses typically meet from 6:00 P.M. to 10:00 P.M. one night a week. (Nonaccelerated weekend courses meet from 9:00 P.M. to 4:00 P.M. on Saturday and Sunday one weekend per month—two months for two units, three months for three units).

Experiential Learning

Since Whitehead's early off-campus programs, the college has recognized the value of students' life experiences not only through offering accelerated courses but also through awarding college credit for experiential learning. In the early 1970s, Whitehead College students could receive twenty-four units of academic credit for five documented years of full-time work experience. In 1979, the college established an assessment center to "oversee the development of university-sponsored evaluation of experiential learning" (Robertson 1997, 20). The center's director created a portfolio system for documenting learning through life and work experiences to be considered for academic credit. (The assessment center does not give credit for life experience. Credit is given for college-level learning and this can be experiential learning.) This new system relied heavily on students' ability to communicate the relevance of their past learning experiences through writing. Because earning credit for learning derived from life experience depended on effective written communication, the portfolio system immediately sent new Whitehead College students a clear message that writing in college is more than an empty exercise: Writing about experiential learning could get them something they want and value—college credit. Assembling the portfolio could also give students the confidence that comes from making new meaning of life experiences they themselves may not have fully valued.

The first students to petition for experiential learning credit through the portfolio system enrolled in a psychology course—Personal and Professional Assessment—in which faculty guided them in compiling a rudimentary version of today's more in-depth portfolio. The current portfolio process is described in an almost two-hundred-page guide that outlines the requirements for earning college credit. Students' portfolios include a resume, an autobiography, experiential learning essays, and proof of university and nonuniversity credit (i.e., formal credit,[5] American Council on Education [ACE] Evaluated Training, and Professional/Certificated Training). To begin generating autobiographies and experiential learning essays that are an integral part of the portfolio, students in Liberal Studies-Environmental Studies enroll in American Visions; Business and Management majors enroll in an elective course, Interpreting Experience; and students in Information Systems take Philosophical Foundations of Management. All three courses have a humanities component, which provides a context for developing portfolios.

Reading and Writing in Experiential Learning Courses. To varying degrees, the experiential learning courses fuse two educational philosophies—one that emphasizes canons of the liberal arts, the other that focuses on students' own experiences and cultures. The twelve-week-long courses include two parts, each taught by a different instructor: a Humanities section that introduces students to intellectual history and worldviews through analyzing texts in the humanities and a Portfolio section that introduces learning theories and guides students in compiling an experiential learning portfolio. In the experiential learning courses, students are challenged to view their experiences through larger lenses of conflicting cultural and philosophical perspectives.[6] As students write experiential learning essays and autobiographies, they examine connections between their own experiences and larger philosophical ideas.

In the American Visions course (six units), students read selections from David Hollinger and Charles Capper's *The American Intellectual Tradition* and other texts to gain an understanding of how "the political, spiritual, and economic visions that have helped shape our culture are themselves cast in such a way as to embody internal tensions and contradictions" (American Visions syllabus). Students examine the tensions in American culture, for example "between individualism and communalism, rationalism and faith, love of nature and drive to development, and egalitarianism and imperialism."

The Interpreting Experience course (three units) revolves less around philosophical conflicts, focusing more on giving students diverse lenses for viewing their own and others' experiences. More course time is devoted to writing autobiographies and experiential learning essays for students' portfolios. The course begins by students' examining their own experiences and then analyzing experiences as represented in academic and literary texts. By the middle of the course, students begin considering competing theoretical frameworks for interpretation in works of literature, sociology, and cultural studies (see Appendix A).

The third experiential learning course, Philosophical Foundations of Management (five units), resembles American Visions more than Interpreting Experience because it focuses on the history of ideas, emphasizing "theories of human nature that underlie management theories" (Management 310 sample syllabus). Students read selections from humanities texts including *Great Ideas* (T. Klein, B. Edwards, and T. Wymer) and *Seven Theories of Human Nature* (L. Stevenson) as they split their time between humanities and portfolio assignments. Reading assignments in *Great Ideas* range from Greek philosophers to Marx, Freud, and Camus.

All three courses culminate in a "diversity assignment" that involves an oral presentation. For this assignment, students are asked to interview "an individual who is as different as possible from [them] in terms of gender, race, religion, class, and ethnic background" or "someone who belongs to an 'invisible' minority—the blind, deaf, or disabled" (Fraiberg 1997, 45). For their presentations, students write an abstract in which they describe "the knowledge they gained from this interview experience" (Fraiberg 1997, 45). This assignment leads students to explore a wide range of influences on interpretive perspectives from language to work ethic, education, religious views and attitudes, sex roles, and lifestyle. The presentation provides the final step in the course-long process of learning to critically interpret texts from the humanities, their own experiences, and the experiences of others.

Along with broad exposure to reading, in the humanities, the experiential learning courses aim to provide students the critical thinking and writing skills they will require to compose autobiographies and experiential learning essays that challenge courses in the University of Redlands catalogue. The courses introduce learning theories such as Bloom's Taxonomy of Educational Objectives and the work of learning theorists such as Kurt Lewin, Ronald Lippit, Ralph K.White, and others. Through writing assignments, students apply these theories, making connections between their past learning experiences and larger philosophical concepts that have currency in academic disciplines. Students' process of translating experiential learning into academic terms is facilitated by work in small groups that provide a "deeper understanding of group interaction" and an opportunity "to break out of the familiar classroom routine into a new kind of learning environment" (*Portfolio Guide* 1997, v–3). The focus on small-group collaboration in the humanities-based writing courses acculturates students to the student-centered pedagogies that characterize most Whitehead College classes.

Working in small groups, students often begin by composing their individual autobiographies—five-page, double-spaced essays that answer the question "Who am I?" in terms of both professional and personal accomplishments. In the *Portfolio Guide* the prompt for the autobiography defines it as a "creative adventure, bound only by the use of proper grammar, collegiate-level exposition, the guidelines set forth by [the] instructor, and finally, by [the student's] own imagination and examination" (1997, v–1). In two samples that appear in the *Portfolio Guide*, the writers outline significant events in their lives that led them to Whitehead College. Both essays give students useful models for narrating their life stories: In the first sample, Barbara Chandler emphasizes a succession of increasingly responsible jobs she has held in the nursing field, interweaving reflections on her personal achievements and losses into her work narrative. The second essay, by Maria Johnston, exhibits a more poetic style, using Paul Gauguin's painting entitled "Where Do We Come From? What Are We? Where Are We Going?" to reflect upon the central role learning has played in her life from her childhood in Italy to her extensive travels and reading experiences as an adult. Whereas these narratives do not in themselves earn students any college credit, they provide the evaluators a larger context for assessing the students' experiential learning essays. Including the autobiographies in the portfolio along with the experiential learning essays also sends the important message to students that their life experience can have value in an academic setting.[7]

Advanced Writing and Critical Analysis

In 1997, Advanced Writing and Critical Analysis was developed to re-place the experiential learning course previously required for Business and Management majors, Philosophical Foundations of Management. Although Business and Management faculty appreciated the rigor of the experiential learning course—often referred to by students as "boot camp"—they wanted to create new required courses in writing and mathematics for their recently redesigned curriculum. Their main pri-orities for the new writing course included preparing students to write critically and analytically, conduct research and document sources, and develop competence in using Standard English grammar. The Business and Management faculty enlisted Fraiberg to design a new course that, in their view, would better prepare their majors for writing and think-ing in upper-division, accelerated courses.

The new course emphasizes writing processes and rhetorical analy-sis, whereas the experiential learning courses draw upon a traditional model of composition instruction, in which students compose many es-says in a relatively short time period rather than working through the kind of recursive writing process advocated by current composition theorists. For example, in American Visions, students might write as many as ten short essays on assigned readings in addition to compos-ing their autobiographies and experiential learning essays. The new Advanced Writing and Critical Analysis course requires three essays that students take through multiple drafts; the last two weeks of the course focus on continued revision, with students choosing two essays to rework again and submit in a revision portfolio.

Along with the focus on writing processes, the new course sub-stitutes the experiential learning courses' focus on critical analysis of philosophical ideas with rhetorical analysis of texts that reflect the theme of Leadership and Influence. In Advanced Writing and Critical Analysis, students analyze essays in Lee A. Jacabus' A *World of Ideas* from rhetorical and thematic points of view, focusing on how the course theme is represented "across time, traditions, and genres as [a] way of understanding the force of language, writing, and communication" (Fraiberg 1997, 4). Writing projects include responses to questions about students' writing histories and processes followed by a series of critical analyses based on readings, with each new analysis requiring more outside research than the one before. Fraiberg's goal is to teach students a rhetorical method for analyzing texts of any genre, whether philosophical texts in the liberal arts tradition or an e-mail message in their place of employment. Therefore, the final essay asks students "to write a critical analysis of a political or philosophical piece that demon-strates the course theme of Leadership and Influence," drawing upon outside research that comments on the text (Fraiberg 1997, 5). For this final assignment, students might analyze "an inaugural speech, a company or university mission statement, a civil rights speech, a keynote address at a major conference, etc." (Fraiberg 1997, 23).

The newly designed course reflects not only Fraiberg's background in composition and rhetoric, but also her desire to tailor the course to the interests of business and management majors while exposing adult students to the liberal arts tradition. Because Fraiberg felt that Business and Management students would spend much time in business and marketing courses analyzing popular culture, she felt it important to begin the advanced course by analyzing historical and philosophical texts that represent the Great Books tradition. Fraiberg noted in an April 10, 1998, interview that many Whitehead faculty members see the liberal arts focus as what sets them apart from adult continuing education programs and "no frills" degree programs that often target working adult students.

At the same time that Fraiberg wanted the advanced writing course to have "a strong philosophical edge," she sought a "trope that would a appeal to [business majors]." Fraiberg found that the theme of Leadership and Influence appeals to upwardly mobile adult students seeking increasingly responsible managerial positions. They enjoy, for instance, tracing Machiavellian influences in their workplace office politics and reading chapters on economics by well-known theorists such as Rousseau and Robert Reich, according to Fraiberg. Because students find these readings challenging and engaging, they practice the critical thinking that the course is designed to teach. As Fraiberg explained, many of the adult students are used to writing reports rather than doing critical analysis that leads to taking and supporting a point of view. Through the Advanced Writing and Critical Analysis course, they practice the critical skills at the heart of liberal studies: the ability to read carefully, draw valid conclusions from their readings, and develop well-constructed arguments that take into account complexities of a text's meanings.

Conclusion

We see the liberal arts-based approach to teaching critical literacy at Whitehead College as the foundation of a rigorous curriculum that accommodates the needs of adult working students without sacrificing the quality of their degree programs. In the experiential learning courses, faculty members balance close readings of liberal arts texts with practice in producing academic discourse through assignments that validate students' experience. The advanced writing course sharpens students' sense of how language works to influence and persuade in various rhetorical situations while introducing them to strategies for research and revision.

In all four writing courses—aside from experiential learning essays and autobiographies that may lead to experiential learning credit—the choice of texts reflects a Great Books approach to education. As Dean Sansing, a strong proponent of a liberal arts education, argued during the March 18 interview, the goal of a liberal arts education is "to alienate people from their normal world." She explained that she "resent[s] very much attempts to make certain liberal arts relevant to working adults" because if teachers are "any good, [students] will make the connection." By valuing students' links between Great Books and their own lives, faculty signal that ideas associated with high culture can be mixed with and inform the everyday culture of work.

The value Whitehead College's writing curricula places on the liberal arts tradition represents one position in an ongoing debate about top-down versus bottom-up approaches to teaching the liberal arts. In "Education Is Politics," Ira Shor critiques the kind of Great Books approach Sansing advocated, which "invents its themes, language, and materials from the top down rather than from the bottom up":

> Faced with unfamiliar scholastic culture, denied an anthropological appreciation of their own culture, students become cultural deficits dependent on the teacher as a delivery system for words, skills, and ideas, to teach them how to speak, think, and act like the dominant elite, whose ways of doing things are the only ones acceptable. (1993, 31)

While Shor rightly identifies the importance of incorporating students' own cultural experiences into course content, Stanley Aronowitz and Henry Giroux defend the top-down approach favored at Whitehead College. In *Education Under Siege*, Aronowitz and Giroux argue that "if students are to be empowered by school experiences, one of the key elements of their education must be that they acquire mastery of language as well as the capacity to think conceptually and critically." To teach critical analysis, they advocate helping students "critically appropriate" the Great Books through close reading and "interrogation of the texts from the perspective of finding the interests, the historical conditions and the tacit assumptions that underlie them as well as the considerable pleasure to be derived from the reading itself" (1985, 158). A second step would be to "ask students to connect their understanding of [the readings] with contemporary issues such as feminism, sexuality and the moral foundations of social order" (1985, 159). By practicing this method of critically appropriating the Great Books, Aronowitz and Giroux argue that students will not see themselves as culturally deficient, as Shor fears. Instead, students will treat the works as one part of a larger definition of popular culture that includes Great Books as well as their own experiences. We see the critical appropriation described by Aronowitz and Giroux as an important goal of Great Books-based writing instruction at Whitehead College. If the courses are successful, for Whitehead College students, the Great Books are no longer separate from their culture but a part of their broadening cultural literacy.

Whitehead College's liberal arts-based approach to education mirrors the whole-man tradition prevalent in union-university adult programs of the '60s and the '70s. Just as the union-university programs emphasized the liberal arts to counteract the trend toward vocationalism, Whitehead attracts and markets itself to adult students who seek professional training along with the prestige and rigor associated with a degree from a small, private liberal arts institution. In this institutional context, we found that writing courses engage students with liberal arts texts to give them the necessary analytical tools for considering issues and ideas through various critical lenses. In the spirit of liberal arts education, the courses seek to prepare students for making enlightened decisions in a democratic society.

Preparing students to make informed decisions in society contrasts with the action orientation of more radical pedagogies originally associated with the labor colleges of the 1920s and '30s and currently advocated by Ira Shor and the late Paulo Freire. At Whitehead College, writing instructors see literacy acquisition as inseparable from ideological critique of the status quo; in fact, many of their programs are designed to meet the needs of the adults who are seeking to succeed in the very corporate culture that radical pedagogies critique. Even so, Whitehead College's faculty and students are participating in a form of resistance that implicitly critiques cultural stereotypes of adult education. Faculty and administrators at Whitehead College believe that their liberal arts-based degree programs for adults counteract a trade-school idea of education, one that ultimately shortchanges working adults and treats them as second-class citizens. Since Whitehead's inception, faculty members have developed rigorous curricula while accommodating the needs of working adults, without sacrificing the quality of their degree programs. Whitehead College provides a useful model for other colleges and universities that seek to balance the larger mission and goals of a liberal arts institution with the training and educational needs of corporations.

Notes

1. For a discussion of issues regarding how distance learning has affected faculty's work life at Whitehead College and elsewhere, see Guthrie, Ruth, Patrick Olson, and Donna M. Schaeffer, "The Professor as Teleworker" in *The*

Virtual Workplace, eds. Magid Igbaria and Margaret Tans (Harrisburg, Pa.: Idea Publishing Group, 1997).

2. Whitehead College employs thirty full-time, tenure-track faculty and approximately four hundred part-time instructors.

3. After a person is certified to teach specific courses through the assessment process, the responsibility for hiring (and rehiring) instructors falls to the college's program directors and "lead" teachers. These full-time, tenure-track faculty play a dual role as academic managers and teachers, developing standard course syllabi, scheduling courses, hiring and evaluating part-time faculty, visiting regional centers, and teaching their own classes.

4. For example, when Fraiburg designed the new Advanced Writing and Critical Analysis course, she stipulated that faculty teaching the course must have at least a masters degree in English or Composition and Rhetoric, experience teaching writing, and knowledge of composition theory.

5. Formal credit includes the following: transfer credits, College Level Examination Program (CLEP), United States Armed Forces Institute (USAFI) tests, Defense Activity for Non-Traditional Educational Support (DANTES) test, and Community College of the Air Force.

6. American Visions meets one evening per week from 6:00 P.M. to 10:00 P.M. for twelve weeks. Philosophical Foundations of Management meets one evening per week from 6:00 P.M. to 10:00 P.M. for ten weeks. Interpreting Experience meets every other Saturday for six hours (9:00 A.M. to 4:00 P.M.) for a total of six days.

7. Specific guidelines for writing the experiential essays appear in the *Portfolio Guide,* including a suggested writing process with emphasis on inventing and developing ideas. The *Portfolio Guide* defines the experiential learning essay as "a documented, student-written narrative of several pages that details college-level experiential learning corresponding to a specific course offered through the University of Redlands" (1997, vi–1). Students are asked to describe in a detailed narrative how they acquired learning that corresponds with the major learning outcomes listed in the college's course catalogue. The *Faculty Guide* for the Interpreting Experience course emphasizes that in their essays, students must strike a balance "between the experiential component and the appropriate theoretical content for the subject matter" (1997, 14).

Chapter Four

Teaching Academic Discourse at Empire State College

In the early 1970s, as the Alfred North Whitehead College began offering extension courses for working adults in Southern California, Empire State College in New York became one of the first public nontraditional institutions of higher education to offer fully accredited degree programs. Founded in 1971 as part of the State University of New York (SUNY) system, Empire State College has expanded to over forty locations and now enrolls approximately ten thousand students and employs 134 full-time, 149 part-time, and numerous adjunct faculty. The school prides itself as a pioneer in offering independent learning programs and college credit for experiential and on-the-job learning (SUNY 1995–1997, 4). Like Whitehead College, Empire State College has built its reputation on offering innovative ways for busy, working people to access the resources of a university, but Empire State College's individualized degree programs give students even more input and control over their courses of study. With no formal departments or programs, students work with faculty mentors to assess their prior learning and current competencies, reflect on their goals, consider possible fields of study, meet with and observe professionals at work in their chosen field, and compose a detailed degree plan.

Empire State College's programs typically attract students between the ages of thirty and fifty, ranging from highly paid corporate executives seeking business degrees to recently laid-off single parents. To serve this diverse student population, Empire State College has regional locations throughout New York state, a growing Center for Distance Learning, and a series of small, specialized programs for individuals or groups with unique needs: FORUM (a bachelor's degree program for

41

experienced managers), Graduate Studies, International Programs, The
Harry Van Arsdale, Jr. School of Labor Studies in Manhattan, the Center for Workforce Advancement, and the SUNY Learning Network for
the Mid-Hudson Region. While each of these programs represents a
significant part of Empire State College, our research centers on writing instruction at the Long Island/Old Westbury and Genesee Valley
centers, the FORUM program, and the Center for Distance Learning
(CDL).[1] Through focusing on these four programs, we learned how
writing instruction is conducted via Empire State College's three main
modes of delivering education—distance learning (at CDL), individual
learning contracts (at the Long Island and Genesee Valley centers), and
residential/individual study (at FORUM).

When we met with faculty at Empire State College centers and programs, we learned Empire State's unique lexicon for describing everything from courses to teachers. Although the Center for Distance
Learning offers courses, other centers offer "guided independent studies" (one-to-one tutorials) and "group studies" (seminar-format workshops on designated topics). Instead of teachers, they have full- and
part-time "primary mentors" (faculty who direct independent, group,
and course studies; they also advise students in setting up and completing degree programs) and "tutors" (adjunct faculty hired to direct
courses, independent studies, or group studies). Rather than syllabi,
faculty work with students to create "learning contracts" (documents
that list assignments, readings, and evaluation criteria for independent
or group studies). Even distance courses are structured so students often have choice and input in assignments. Finally, rather than conventional letter grades, Empire State students receive written evaluations
of their work for each independent or group study.

Based on visits to two regional centers, discussions with faculty
and administrators at the coordinating center in Saratoga Springs, New
York, and examination of course materials and other documents, we
found that approaches to teaching writing at Empire State vary widely
depending upon the route students take toward their degrees and the
unique culture of each of the forty centers. Even though no coherent,
overarching philosophy links writing instruction in different programs,
writing plays an integral role in all Empire State College degrees. This
chapter describes the range of theoretical approaches to teaching writing employed at the Empire State sites we visited, approaches that
range from a feminist expressionist pedagogy for business executives
to a cognitivist approach for adult distance learning students. Regard-
less of the theoretical framework informing faculty's approaches to
teaching writing, we found that faculty all stress the importance of students learning academic discourse as the key to success at Empire State
College.

Writing Across the Curriculum
via Independent Studies

Most writing instruction at Empire State College takes place through group studies, individual tutoring, and frequent writing assignments by cross-disciplinary faculty. To better understand how faculty in different disciplines teach writing through independent study, we attended a faculty meeting at Empire State's Long Island Center. The former director of the center, Silvia Chelala, explained that everyone in the room was a teacher of writing in addition to being an expert in one of the eleven areas of study available at Empire State College.[2] The cross-disciplinary faculty we spoke with seemed interested in learning strategies for using writing more effectively in their independent studies. During the course of an hour, we discussed goals of writing instruction with faculty from philosophy and religion, community and human services, art, linguistics, history, psychology, business management, sociology, physics, computer science, political science, mathematics, English, and education. Each faculty member in the room had a stake in the conversation since all full- and part-time mentors teach a study called Educational Planning in which students design their degree plans. Because the degree plan must include a "rationale"—a four- to six-page essay justifying the student's course of study within the state of New York guidelines—students immediately "have reason to write, and [mentors] have a reason to try and help them," according to a June 17, 1997, interview with Chelala.

As faculty members shared their frustrations and successes with teaching writing to adult students, several of them explained their strategies for introducing students to discourse used in their disciplinary conversations. In an interview on June 17, 1997, Jim Robinson, a history and political science professor, said he sees his first task as "getting students to articulate," by which he means expressing their ideas and developing a voice. He explained that he wants students "to understand the general range of cultural ideas in history and political science, but what's important are their ideas." To achieve that goal, especially with students who have little or no college experience, he developed a study titled Introduction to Analytical Reasoning. In this study, he asks students to read four fiction or nonfiction books, write summaries of the books, and meet with him to discuss what they found meaningful. Robinson's job is "to listen carefully and hear what they're driving at," repeat their ideas back to them, and assign them to write about their ideas. Ultimately, his goal is help students move to higher levels of abstraction and elaboration by asking students to take a position and elaborate on their point of view so that they can persuade him "that what they have to say is reasonable." In all his courses, Robinson attunes himself to each student's confidence level and familiarity with academic discourse, helping them with self-expression before "getting them to deal with the formalities of the discipline." He says the purpose of his job is "to raise the level of formal conversation as we go along . . . [seeing] that it doesn't stay on the level of self-expression, of anecdotal narrative."

Another strategy for easing students into disciplinary-based writing was described in a June 17, 1997, interview by Barbara Kantz and Evelyn Wells, two Community and Human Services professors. Since many of their students work in human services and "are interested in the stories of other people," Kantz builds on that interest by having them write narratives about themselves or their clients. Kantz finds that autobiographical writing provides a useful bridge to more disciplinary-based writing. When working with students, she often tape-records what they say, asking them to "tell me this book"; then she plays back what they say, explaining "that's what [you] should be writing." Kantz uses this exercise to show students that they need not "get caught up in thinking they have to translate" their ideas and experiences into what they perceive as college-level language.

Kantz, Wells, and Robinson all focus first on getting students comfortable with expressing their ideas in a familiar form; later they help students develop strategies for presenting ideas through disciplinary conventions. This sensitivity that faculty at the Long Island Center show in helping students make a transition from their "everyday" oral and written literacies to written disciplinary discourse may reflect the context in which they teach—a college dedicated to serving nontraditional adult students. The faculty's flexible, creative approaches to teaching writing across the disciplines complements the larger college philosophy that students' needs should drive curriculum and pedagogy.

First-Year Writing Instruction at the Genesee Valley Center

In addition to the decentralized writing instruction offered by cross-disciplinary faculty at all the Empire State College centers, Empire State College's first organized, comprehensive writing program was created by a mentor at the Genesee Valley Center, Herbert Shapiro. Shapiro aims to professionalize the teaching of writing at Empire State College by connecting Empire State to the larger composition community and creating communities of writers within Empire State College's individual learning model, according to an interview on October 31, 1997.

While Shapiro believes students receive excellent instruction in mentor-directed studies, he also recognizes the intellectual and emotional value of students learning from one another. Since most Empire State College students work independently, they miss out on the kind of support systems built into traditional degree programs. They often lack opportunities to check their progress in relation to their peers, to form networks that provide emotional support, or to participate in collaborative learning. To solve this problem, Shapiro created a peer tutoring program modeled after Kenneth Bruffee's program at Brooklyn College. Students learn about the peer tutoring program at an orientation, where they also provide a writing sample that Shapiro assesses holistically and uses to recommend the appropriate writing program support services—either group studies in composition, individualized studies in basic writing skills, or noncredit workshops, Shapiro said in the interview.

Many of the best writers who also display the personal qualities required for effective tutoring are invited to become peer tutors. Schooled in a range of composition theories before they begin scheduling tutorials, peer tutors work "in the middle," as Muriel Harris uses the phrase: bridging gaps between students and faculty and between home and academic discourse.[3] So that tutors can work effectively in the middle, Shapiro urges them to define "the discourse of higher education" for themselves. Once tutors develop their own definitions of academic discourse, he introduces them to terminology from Linda Flower's "Negotiating Academic Discourse." He points out how Flower's "critical thinking," a "non-personal voice," and "a sense of objective conclusions" provide useful starting points for discussing academic language with peers who visit the writing center. Through helping tutors learn a metalanguage for talking about academic discourse, Shapiro seeks to create a community of learners who guide one another in the transition from their "home" literacies to the languages of the university, according to the interview.

One of Shapiro's success stories is a tutor who comes from a blue-collar background, who went through the tutor-training program, worked as a tutor, and plans to pursue doctoral studies in English at a prestigious graduate school. This example underscores Shapiro's commitment "to [meeting] each student at the level or place he or she is at and [knowing] that [he] can bring that person to someplace different— not necessarily better but different." Through the writing center and his own teaching, Shapiro said he seeks to create a community of learners and educators who help each other reap the rewards of academic success—a college degree, promotion at the workplace, and communication skills needed for effective citizenship.

Shapiro's peer tutoring program at Genesee Valley is built on the premise that academic discourse is best learned through a social process. Simultaneously, he is influenced by a cognitivist approach in his extensive use of Flower's social-cognitivist models of composing and definitions of academic discourse. Shapiro demonstrates an effective marriage of social and cognitivist approaches to writing instruction in his peer tutoring program, in which students guide one another in a collaborative, systematic process of understanding the expectations of academic discourse communities. While Shapiro does not guide students through critiques of academic discourse as radical educators might, he does move toward a critical approach by explaining to students that academic discourse, in its various forms, is only one of many valid discourses invested with power by particular communities.

FORUM/East Program: Saratoga Springs

While mentors at Long Island and peer tutors at Genesee Valley focus on helping students find their own voices in academic discourse, Elaine Handley, a mentor in the FORUM/East Program at Saratoga Springs, complicates this goal by urging students to experiment with academic and creative forms of writing. Handley, who develops writing and literature studies, explained in an interview on October 20, 1997, that most FORUM/East students are Bell Atlantic employees in their forties who come from working-class backgrounds, have worked their way up into managerial positions, and earn between sixty thousand dollars and one hundred thousand dollars a year. She described students as "bright and motivated" people seeking degrees to keep their jobs or to stay marketable in the climate of corporate downsizing. Most students enter the program with prior college credit or associates degrees, which might include a college writing course taken ten or twenty years ago. Because most students' writing experience has been limited to writing lists, letters, and memos on the job, Handley noted that they often need more writing practice to succeed in Empire State College's writing-intensive degree program.

Writing Consultants

Handley first meets her students at an orientation session, where new FORUM students pick up course materials and meet their mentors. According to the interview with Handley, "At orientation we have to do a little persuasion about why writing is important. We immediately start talking to them about how writing is a process—a vehicle for developing ideas. We urge them to study writing at the beginning of their degree program." To underscore the importance of writing, Handley and all FORUM mentors assign each new student a writing consultant—professional writers whom FORUM hires to work one-on-one with students (mentors in FORUM hoped the term "consultant" would appeal to business people). One of the consultants, currently a playwright, formerly wrote speeches for the CEO of J.C. Penney Company; the other one, a journalist by training, writes novels. These writers teach a group study and they consult individually with students about drafts, thesis statements, revision strategies, or papers deemed unacceptable by mentors or tutors. Consultants meet with students face to face at each residency or by phone, e-mail, mail, or fax between residencies. Handley explained that "if [students are] struggling with the writing, there is absolutely no reason for them to struggle alone and not get the kind of support and help they need."[4]

Through referring students to writing consultants, FORUM mentors recognize the importance of students' writing processes; through *The FORUM Chronicle,* a publication of student and faculty work, they celebrate students' final products. Published twice a year, the *Chronicle* anthologizes fiction, personal essays, drama, academic essays, interviews, poetry, drawings, and commencement addresses. Also, Excellence in Writing awards, as well as the *Chronicle*'s Reader's Choice Awards, underscore the importance of writing, and students feel empowered by seeing their writing in print, according to Handley.

Theme Study and Residencies. Students in the FORUM program meet with writing consultants and mentors during weekend-long "residencies" as part of their guided independent studies. The standard residency involves a three-hour class, thirty- to forty-five-minute individual conferences, and a three-hour student debate, discussion, or writing workshop. Residencies take place in hotel conferences rooms and typically involve six to fifteen students. Before the first of three residencies, mentors mail out at least one assignment so that students come to the first meeting "having already done a fair amount of reading and writing" Handley said in the October 20, 1997, interview. Handley runs her residency sessions like a student-centered class, encouraging each student to speak early on, hoping to make them feel comfortable about participating further. Students spend much of the time writing, beginning with freewriting, which they read aloud to the group. In the second and third residencies, students bring writing to read aloud for peer response.

Residencies comprise a key component of the one required study in the FORUM program, a two-semester Theme Study. In this writing-intensive study, students are assigned a current topic relevant to the business world—a recent theme was the role of business in public school reform. In the first semester, students research, write about, and discuss their assigned topics through individual study and the weekend residencies. For the first-semester residencies, students meet for one and a half hours on Friday and Saturday night and three hours on Sunday, "becoming experts on the issue, discussing it, researching, starting to strategize." During the second-semester residencies, they spend three hours publicly debating another team that has been researching the same topic. Through this process, which Handley calls "intense, exciting, and energizing," students practice public speaking, collaboration, and research.

Overall, Handley's approach to strengthening students' writing might be characterized as feminist expressionism. Rather than focusing on problem solving, audience, and form (as many students expect), her writing courses encourage self-exploration and often incorporate gender and multicultural themes. Handley's interest in women's studies and her training in the liberal arts tradition shape her belief that FORUM students need exposure to ideas that expand their perspectives beyond the corporate world. Through assigning feminist texts by authors such as Alice Walker and Charlotte Perkins Gilman, she raises gender issues that many of the managers, both male and female, have not previously considered. She also introduces students to a range of writing genres, encouraging them to experiment with creative and academic forms of writing. At the same time, she includes business-oriented self-help texts that directly relate to the corporate world but emphasize self-fulfillment through creatively integrating personal life and work (for an example, see one of her recent learning contracts titled "Our Working Lives: Writing for Meaning" in Appendix B). Through all the readings she assigns, whether they are business or liberal arts texts, she hopes, through reading and writing, to "advance the quality of [her students'] lives," according to the interview.

Center for Distance Learning (CDL)

Housed in the Saratoga Springs Coordinating Center along with the FORUM program is Empire State's Center for Distance Learning. The center was founded in the mid-1970s to serve students who find that even Empire State College's flexible approach to guided independent study does not fit their needs. Today, the college's CDL enrolls between two thousand and three thousand students from New York and around the country. CDL students take fifteen-week courses, in which approximately fifteen to twenty-five students work through a standardized course with a tutor, whom they contact by phone, fax, mail, and e-mail.

In an interview on October 21, 1997, Susan Oaks, the area coordinator for Communications, Arts, and Humanities, distinguished between traditional correspondence courses and the CDL's approach to distance education. Oaks explained that to effectively teach students the writing skills they need, the term "distance learning" must not be taken literally. She discourages use of the term because it implies distance from instruction and from other students. Unlike correspondence courses, in which students work in isolation, Empire State College's delivery method fosters connections with faculty via phone and e-mail. Students receive a letter and course materials through the mail followed by a phone call from the tutor and mentor. During this call, students and faculty get to know each other, discuss the course, and agree upon dates for subsequent phone contact. Between phone calls, students rely on the carefully structured course guides—ranging from twenty to more than one hundred pages in length—to coach them through the process of completing assignments.

While this print-based approach to distance learning has been the primary mode of delivery, the CDL has also begun making a transition to World Wide Web-based courses, which may allow for even more student-student and student-faculty interaction. Recently, Oaks, Handley, and Cathy Copley-Woods worked to create an on-line writing center, The Writer's Complex. This virtual writing center offers Empire State College students information at a click, corridors to discuss writing with other students, and e-mail access to a tutor. Through a system of hypertextual links, the Writer's Complex "fosters a kind of transitional community, a support group, that conjoins the conventions, values, goals, and interests of students' 'home' discourse communities and those of academy." To create a virtual community that nurtures adult students who may feel "intimidated by academia," the voices students encounter on-line take a personal or subjective tone rather than "simply presenting objective principles and rules for good college papers," wrote Copley-Woods in a personal correspondence dated June 4, 1998. Through this on-line writing center, Empire State College faculty hope to capitalize on the Internet's potential for recreating the social interaction that students at traditional institutions experience both inside and outside the classroom.[5]

Writing Instruction Through Distance Education

Because Oaks supervises tutors and has primary responsibility for writing and revising course guides, her philosophy of writing has strongly influenced the program as a whole.[6] Oaks characterized Empire State College's distance learning courses as process-oriented, student-centered, apolitical courses that prepare students to write clearly and competently in future courses and on the job. In describing her pedagogy as apolitical, she emphasized her strong belief that student-centered pedagogies must put students' experiences and agendas at the center of a course. In her view, political perspectives advocated by tutors or composition readers impinge on students' freedom to set their own agendas and choose their own writing topics. As a result, she uses textbooks featuring student writing on a variety of topics and avoids thematic courses and readers focusing on multicultural or educational issues.

Oaks' approach to teaching writing contrasts with Handley's feminist expressionism. Whereas Handley seeks to raise students' consciousness about issues of difference, Oaks eschews an overt political agenda. And while Handley sees language mainly as a vehicle for self-exploration and expression, Oaks takes a more objectivist view of language, one that places a premium on clarity and conventional forms as opposed to experimentation with form.[7] An objectivist perspective infuses her description of the goals for the CDL writing courses: "Essentially, when student[s] graduate we want them to be able to use language correctly and clearly; they will have had to learn essay format —what is an essay?—thesis, analytical writing, and they will have learned documentation—the bottom line, bare bones of academic writing," Oaks said in the October 21 interview. We see "cognitive rhetoric" as a dominant strand in Oaks' approach to teaching writing: The CDL courses she designs teach students systematic, goal-oriented reading and writing processes, with the end result being mastery of discursive practices valued in the academic and corporate worlds.

*a cognitive /
objectivist
approach*

Educational Planning and College Writing Courses. Oaks shared with us a copy of the *Educational Planning Guide* for the first part of the two-semester, writing-intensive course that takes students through a process of self-assessment culminating in their degree plans. The guide, coauthored by Thomas Dehner, includes numerous inventories and short writing exercises, along with three essay assignments (each three to five pages in length): a learning portrait essay, an essay on education, and an essay on learning goals (see Appendix C).

The step-by-step process outlined in the guide breaks down the goal of writing a learning portrait essay into discrete, manageable units. In a course overview at the front of the booklet, students are introduced to the first of four questions that frame the course and become a heuristic for the essay assignments and the larger project of creating a degree plan.[8] To answer Question 1—What do I know/not know/want to know?—students first do an inventory of their skills and knowledge in eight areas such as observation, critical analysis, quantitative reasoning, communication skills, and time management. Responses to questions on a series of inventories become the basis for the learning portrait essay, their first major writing assignment (see Appendix C).

Each of the subsequent assignments takes students through a similarly systematic process of analysis and writing. The essay on education assignment, however, attempts the additional goal of moving students outside "the realm of individual, abstract thought" and introducing them to the idea that knowledge is socially and culturally constructed. To illustrate that a person's knowledge is not "complete if it exists only in the realm of individual, abstract thought," Oaks and Dehner ask students to research "what constitutes an educated person in the U.S. today?" Students then compare their findings with "the thoughts of professional educators, the people who set and enact educational policy."[9] After analyzing the main purpose of the educators' arguments and the values underlying their stances, students identify how their points of view compare with those of the professional educators. The assignment concludes with students writing an essay giving their own informed opinion about what qualities higher education should be promoting in students or writing a position paper in response to an article on the purpose of higher education. Each of these options is designed to prepare students for writing the final essay, in which they explain their personal learning goals by synthesizing all the self-assessment work they have done in Educational Planning (Oaks and Dehner 1996, 95).[10]

The essay on education assignment delineates Oaks' cognitive approach to rhetoric tinged with a more social perspective. That is, students are encouraged to see their own ideas about learning in relation to larger educational and professional contexts. Overall, the guide's systematic approach to writing and analysis models a cognitive process that the authors urge students to learn and apply as a template to other situations that call for writing, decision making, or self-assessment. For students who need more practice in writing, they will most immediately apply the metacognitive strategies developed in Educational Planning in their first CDL writing course, usually either Introduction to College Reading and Writing or College Writing.

Conclusion

Despite the differing approaches to writing instruction at Empire State College, faculty share a deep commitment to adapting curricula to adult learners. They believe in providing a space for adult students to explore their own experiences through writing to validate what they know and make them comfortable, according to the October 21, 1997, interview with Oaks. The faculty we interviewed understand the anxieties that most adult students, especially those from working-class backgrounds, bring to college writing. Faculty most concerned with social factors devised innovative strategies for meeting students where they are in terms of their oral and written communication skills. At the same time, Empire State College faculty agree that students must eventually present their ideas in the diction, style, and organizational patterns expected in disciplinary and workplace writing.

This emphasis on teaching the conventions of academic writing as a means to success reflects the school's targeted audience of working adults who seek career advancement through education. Empire State College shares Whitehead College's goal of facilitating social mobility and preparing students to adapt to a changing workplace. However, underlying this relatively conservative goal is the more progressive philosophy that working adults should have the freedom to craft their own education. In their educational planning studies, students take on a Freirean project of investigating what different models of education have to offer and making their own choices. As a result, Empire State College's student-centered approach to education offers rich possibilities for working adults to participate in a potentially liberating educational process.

Notes

1. We chose these sites in part because of convenience—for instance, we could visit the Long Island Center at the same time as the Queens College Extension Center, the subject of Chapter 5.

2. Because Empire State College does not have a set curriculum, they have developed eleven broad areas of study: The Arts; Business, Management, and Economics; Community and Human Services; Cultural Studies; Educational Studies; Historical Studies; Human Development; Labor Studies; Science, Mathematics, and Technology; Social Theory, Social Structure, and Change; and Interdisciplinary Studies.

3. See Muriel Harris, "Talking in the Middle: Why Writers Need Writing Tutors," *College English* 57.1 (January 1995): 27–43 for a discussion of the significance of this term.

4. According to Handley, the consultants take a "practical" approach that appeals to the FORUM students. In Donald Murray fashion, these practicing writers offer advice and tips for generating ideas, writing to particular audiences, and meeting deadlines. While the consultant's down-to-earth approach complements the students' own practical bent, students reluctantly use their services because they find it difficult to admit that they need help. Since the consultants are readily available, Handley found students' reluctance to contact them puzzling. When they explained that admitting "ignorance" on the job signaled incompetence, she saw that they had been transferring corporate values to the academic setting. They told her, "If we admit we're weak in something, we just sold ourselves down the river." To overcome their hesitation about getting help, Handley tells students at orientation that in the academic setting, faculty see it as a sign of strength for students to ask for help when they don't know something.

5. The Writer's Complex introduces students to the conventions of academic discourse, often via organic metaphors for composing, colorful graphics, and jargon-free explanations that reflect Handley's expressionism. The Writer's Complex can be found at http://www.esc.edu/writer.htm.

6. Oaks carefully selects and supervises the twenty tutors who teach courses in her area. Since students depend on a tutor's comments to revise their writing, the tone and content become even more important than in a traditional classroom-based course. All tutors submit to Oaks copies of the three-part summative and formative comments they are expected to give students for every assignment. At midterm and at the end of the course, Oaks reviews responses and gives tutors feedback on the appropriateness of their summary comments, which follow a "sandwich" format—"good things first, what could be improved in middle, a supportive comment at the end" (interview, October 21, 1997).

7. As Berlin (1987) explains in *Rhetoric and Reality,* an objectivist view of language assumes that there is a rational world apart from language that can be understood by individual minds, translated into language, and understood by other individual minds. In contrast, social constructionists view language as shaping a world that can only partially be known by individual minds. Instead, they hold that what we know of the constructed world is mediated by factors such as the various discourse communities we are part of, our historical and cultural moment, and our socially constructed identities (influenced by race, class, gender, age, etc.).

8. The following are the four questions that frame the course: (1) What do I know/not know/want to know? (2) What do I need to know and why? (3) What are my skills/resources for learning? and (4) What are the implications for future learning? (Oaks and Dehner 1996, 5).

9. Although the course guide includes several articles, students are required to read "A Minimum Required Curriculum" (from the Association of American Colleges' report on *Integrity in the College Curriculum*) and "Vocational and General Education: New Relationship or Shotgun Marriage" (from *New Directions for Community Colleges*). Students also may opt to explore cultural differences in higher education, thus extending their notions of context beyond the United States.

10. After writing the essay on education, students have the option of doing an in-depth writing self-assessment (along with assessments in other areas). To do the writing assessment, students work through a separate booklet, in which they answer multiple-choice questions on grammar, usage, and punctuation and write a short analytical essay. The booklet provides sample essays with comments explaining the degree to which each sample represents "the basic characteristics of analytical college writing" (Oaks 1991, 41). To assess their preparation for college writing, students compare their essay to the samples and examine it in light of a list of criteria for college writing. The criteria list includes a series of questions about grammar, diction, detail, thesis, paragraphing, organization, coherence, and level of analysis (for the sake of brevity, we have used terms such as "thesis" and "diction" to describe the criteria, which the booklet avoids in favor of non-

technical language). After working through the step-by-step process, students use assessment worksheets to determine the areas of writing in which they need more practice. Finally, in consultation with their advisors, they decide what CDL writing course they will take or whether they should take a noncredit writing tutorial (another option is for students to seek "remedial" help from a community or literacy program in their own community).

Chapter Five

Critical Literacy in Action
Queens College Worker
Education Program

Three programs exist under the umbrella of the Queens College Worker Education Program: the Labor Education and Advancement Project (LEAP), the longest-standing program, designed to serve worker-students on the Queens campus; the Worker Education Extension Center in Manhattan, created to offer students another location for taking courses; and the Labor Resource Center, developed to serve the research and educational needs of the labor movement and the community.[1] All three programs respond to needs of the labor community and take labor studies as their intellectual bases. The Extension Center program dates back to 1976 when it was run by Hofstra University in affiliation with UAW District 65. Queens College acquired the program in 1991, and led by Extension Center Director Sean Sweeney, began developing degree programs that maintain the spirit of the Hofstra mission—"to provide higher educational opportunities for working adults with an emphasis on the liberal arts, the social sciences, and leadership development."[2] To some degree, continuity between the two programs was maintained by Sweeney, who joined the Hofstra program in 1988. He brought from Hofstra a commitment to "a collectivist and solidaristic approach to learning, [in which] traditional modes of teaching/learning were openly criticized and even condemned for their classist, racist, sexist, homophobic, and all-round oppressive character," according to a personal correspondence dated June 10, 1998.

Our research focuses on the writing program at the Queens College Extension Center, which was established in 1991 in Manhattan and currently serves students who are union stewards, garment workers, government employees, and health care workers. Of the 150 students at Queens College Extension Center, 97 percent are minorities, mostly African American women with increasing numbers of Latino students.[3]

Through examining course materials, grant reports, and speaking with the program director, faculty, and a student counselor, we found that the writing instruction students receive at the Manhattan Center is grounded in an activist critical literacy. Assignments integrate problem posing, critical analysis, and creative writing as students compose for a wide variety of audiences, often for the purpose of enacting change through collective action in organizations and communities. These action-oriented assignments reflect the Worker Education Program's larger mission of developing students' analytical and critical habits of mind so that they can take on new and increasingly active roles in work and community affairs. As this chapter shows, the writing curricula also carry the strong imprint of a small group of adjunct faculty who teach the writing courses, each bringing to the program diverse teaching histories that include experience with Freirean radical pedagogies.

Adaptations to Students' Needs

Queens College Worker Education Program began in 1984 through a collaboration between the college and three unions: Local 1180 of the Communications Workers of America, the New York Joint Board of ACTWU, and Local 1549 of District Council 37, AFSCME. When the program began on the Queens campus, fifty-two students enrolled. Since the 1980s the program has experienced a steady growth with fourteen unions offering tuition reimbursements or scholarships for union members who enroll in the Worker Education Program (currently, enrollment nears six hundred students). Gregory Mantsios, the director of the Office of Worker Education, stressed in a June 19, 1997, interview that "from the first day, we [administrators and faculty] worked very hard to try to set up a community within the college that would meet the needs of working adult students."[4] To shape such a community, the Worker Education Program has sought to elicit worker-students' input in several ways, such as having students interview prospective faculty members or serve on the Queens College Academic Senate. Students' needs are also represented by members of the program's Labor Advisory Board, a group that includes labor leaders from a wide variety of the city's unions. A continuing dialogue with the labor community and with students themselves has resulted in a program that provides worker-students financial and academic support, a special admissions process, and an innovative curriculum emphasizing working-class experience, writing, labor studies, social issues, and community activism.

Admissions Requirements, Financial Assistance, and Academic Support

In creating the Worker Education Program, the rigorous admission policy at Queens College posed the first hurdle. Often referred to as "the jewel" of the city university system, Queens College typically expects a B+ high school grade point average in a college preparatory curriculum, along with strong test scores, especially for GED recipients. Candidates for the Worker Education Program come from a variety of nontraditional backgrounds and often lack the academic credentials Queens requires for admission. As Mantsios pointed out in the interview, when the program began, it attracted a "mixed bag of students: On one hand, we had supervisors and clerical support people from the welfare offices and other government agencies who had a relatively high level of written communication skills. And on the other hand, we had garment workers who worked in factories all day and who were really thrilled to have the opportunity to return to school but who lacked some basic skills needed to succeed on the college level. Many of them were the first ones in their family to go to school. Some had slaved to get their own kids through school, and this was now their opportunity."

To make Queens College accessible for these students, Mantsios and others made a series of arguments to the administration, pointing out, for instance, that high school grades were "largely irrelevant in telling us who our students are and what they're capable of doing at this stage in their life," according to the June 19 inteview. They further asserted that workers differed from traditional students because they can "draw on their life in the learning process" and at the same time "enrich the classroom, the learning experience, and the college as a result of that experience." When these working students had gaps in their academic preparation, Mantsios explained that the Worker Education Program "would be able to provide a different structure and support system" to bridge these gaps. This support system was to be financed through outside grants, for example from the statewide Consortium for Worker Education. Convinced by these arguments, the administration ultimately agreed to a kind of "dual track" system since they couldn't justify having different standards for traditional and nontraditional students. For admission to the Worker Education Program, students had to be over twenty-five years old, highly motivated, and willing to put in extra time to get "up to speed" in any areas that may need more work.

Presently, the dual track system that opened access to working adults is being threatened by a CUNY Board of Trustees decision to enforce a 1985 policy that requires all CUNY students to pass assessment tests in math, writing, and reading prior to admission. As Sweeney explained in the June 10 correspondence, these assessment tests pose a "very serious obstacle" to working adult students, who already take an average of over seven years to graduate. Requiring additional remedial work before allowing students to take courses for credit will result in many working adults "turning their backs on college."

Adapted admissions criteria, along with academic and financial support from grants and union tuition reimbursement have played key roles in "open[ing] up a fairly elite school to workers," according to Mantsios in the June 19 interview. Workers who meet the adapted admission requirements typically receive tuition reimbursement from their unions for classes in which they earn a grade of C or better. If worker-students need academic support, grants from the Consortium for Worker Education, the CUNY Consortium for Disability Studies, and the CWA/CUNY Alliance have enabled the program to provide academic counseling, access to a computer lab, and individual tutoring in reading, math, and writing (see section on Basic Writing Workshops later in this chapter). This support system helps bring students to the necessary level to complete their degree program rather than compromising the high standards of Queens College.

Queens College's high standards make the Manhattan-based extension program particularly attractive to union leaders, whose financial and political backing helped create the program and ensure its continued existence.[5] As Mantsios explained, "When we first discussed a union-based program, labor leaders made it clear that they did not want to start a program at a school that would be easy to get into and easy to get through, so they made the decision to go with a school that had tough standards. Our position has always been that we are not going to water down standards; instead, we bring students to where they need to be." Mantsios explained how, for him, one immigrant student's experience illustrates the exceptional opportunity the Worker Education Program provides motivated students who take advantage of all support offered to help students succeed:

> One of our students, Hector, was a tie maker. He sewed labels onto ties all day in a very hot, awful factory out in Long Island City. The program with his union was only set up to cover his tuition for a B.A. degree, but he was one of these guys who came in and did fifteen credits a semester and aced all his credits. He then convinced the union to allow him to pursue a master's degree on these same funds . . . So he became a school teacher. With the education he received, he just completely changed his life around.

Hector's educational odyssey was made possible by his own motivation and hard work combined with an impressive collaboration between the Queens College administration, the Worker Education Program, and labor unions.

Worker-Centered, Writing-Intensive Curriculum

While working adults typically bring strong motivation and excellent verbal skills to their course work, their writing performance often lags behind their verbal and cognitive abilities, according to a June 20, 1997, interview with Lucienne Muller, academic counselor for the Worker Education Program. Working with writing instructors, Muller initiated discussions with faculty in American Studies and Sociology about how to teach writing in content courses. They discussed the importance of giving a series of short writing assignments rather than one large project at the end of the course and encouraged faculty to identify early in the term students who needed extra help with writing. Through shorter, more manageable essays, Muller feels students can more easily "find their own voice" rather than just piecing text together from different sources. For a Sociology professor, revising her course to integrate writing more effectively meant using "small articles instead of a textbook" and dealing with concepts in the class through as many as ten one-and-a-half-page writing assignments.

This writing-intensive approach, according to Muller, makes some students uncomfortable because they hadn't expected to have to confront their difficulties with writing outside of the required writing courses. Even so, Muller and others believe that the only way for students to become more comfortable and confident in their writing is to continue integrating writing instruction throughout the curriculum. Therefore, as the Queens Extension Center begins the process of redesigning their curriculum, the revision will include even more writing across the curriculum, along with continued support for students who need extra tutoring and workshops in reading and writing, according to the interview with Muller.

Writing Instructors

The union-based nature of Queens program has attracted writing instructors with strong commitments to teaching working adults, knowledge of the labor movement's history, an activist bent, and experience with radical pedagogies. Although all the writing teachers in the Worker Education Program work as adjunct faculty, unlike Whitehead's staff of part-time teachers, these faculty are fewer in number, have great autonomy in designing courses, and collaborate with one another in curriculum design.

Of the three writing teachers at the Queens Extension, Norah Chase has the longest history with the program, dating back to the late 1970s when she taught in the Hofstra-District 65 program. Currently a full-time faculty member in English at Kingsburough Community College, another institution in the CUNY system, she teaches part of her required hours at the Queens Extension Program. Despite her adjunct status, Chase's active, long-term involvement in worker education at Queens has contributed to creating the kind of stimulating teaching and learning environment that is often difficult to maintain in programs that rely exclusively on part-time faculty. Chase brings to her teaching a background in radical and feminist pedagogy that leads her to make connections between education and social responsibility and to seek out collaborative teaching situations through paired, interdisciplinary classes, according to an interview with her on October 3, 1997. Her interest in paired courses made her a natural choice for coordinating the Extension Center's Solidarity Project. This curriculum initiative, made possible by a CUNY New Visions Grant, involved creating paired courses in writing and labor studies at the Queens Worker Education Program.

The writing teacher selected to participate in the Solidarity Project, Cara Murray, teaches a range of composition and journalism courses at the Extension Center. Murray's background in journalism, English, and economics have been the major influences on her teaching of writing. While her approach to teaching is more literary than political in the first-year writing courses, she brought an overt political agenda to the Article and Newspaper Writing class she taught for the Solidarity Project (the course focused on the Welfare Employment Program and the economics of work in the garment industry). According to an October 14, 1997, interview, Murray's rationale for making her own political views part of the curriculum comes from her belief that we are all "shaped by this world in some way." She points out that her pro-labor economic perspective is "probably more than anything shaped by what happened to Pittsburgh in the '70s, seeing a community go from being vibrant to being nothing, and the mass sort of depression that followed the pull out of the steel mills." While she struggles with the issue of how best to include her own political views in the classroom, for now she believes that the key is to be "honest with your students about where you're coming from" and not "penalize the students" who hold a different viewpoint. Murray's evolving sense of the writing classroom as a site of political debate and action continues to be refined through ongoing conversations about activist pedagogy with her colleagues at the Extension Center.

A frequent participant in conversations about politics and the classroom, Emily Schnee was recently hired as the full-time coordinator of Developmental Skills through funding from the Consortium for Worker Education. Schnee's job involves running workshops on reading and writing and doing individual tutoring. Her approach to teaching writing has been shaped by her work with a literacy campaign in Nicaragua, her involvement in the New York City Writing Project, graduate courses in composition theory, her years of teaching in union-based adult education programs, and her own union activism. From her work in the Nicaraguan literacy program, Schnee feels that "in the most fundamental ways my ideas about education have been influenced by the Freirean goal of getting students to think critically and act upon the world," according to an interview on July 21, 1997. Schnee models for working adults a life of reflective action through her own union activism. For her, active union membership means not only actively supporting her union, but also using the tools of critical reading and writing to analyze its actions and if necessary to critique them.

Basic Writing Workshops

Before Schnee was hired at the Queens Extension Center, a series of adjunct faculty were responsible for "developmental" work in reading and writing. Students are placed in these developmental workshops as a result of failing the CUNY Writing Assessment Test (WAT), a three-hour standardized test that students at all city colleges of the university must pass by the time they finish their sixtieth credit. (CUNY's recent decision to enforce the 1985 Board of Trustees policy will change this sixtieth credit rule, forcing students to pass the test before admission.) When Schnee joined the faculty full time, she brought a much-needed continuity to the program: Students could get to know her, and she could work with them over an extended period of time. Schnee's background in critical literacy education gave her strategies for working effectively with and against the controversial institutional constraint posed by the WAT. Aware of the considerable anxiety the test produces in her students, Schnee uses a controversy surrounding the WAT as a Freirean generative theme in her reading and writing workshops at the Extension Center. Topics such as the WAT controversy, which could be explored under larger themes of education or literacy, appeal to Schnee because she believes that they tap into working students' desire to explore identities that go beyond being a worker. At the same time, she leaves spaces in her courses for students' own ideas and agendas to emerge and become part of the course curriculum.

In a typical workshop-tutorial, attended by nine to thirteen students, Schnee might begin by taking students through a composing process recommended by Sondra Perl and facilitators of the New York City Writing Project. After moving students through a series of invention techniques, she gleans from their writing relevant issues that might become part of the workshop's curriculum. In the samples Schnee shared with us, students wrote about past experiences with literacy, responses to readings, and educational issues. Schnee also introduces students to theories about writing through excerpts from Peter Elbow's *Writing Without Teachers* and Natalie Goldberg's *Writing Down the Bones*, asking them to implement those theories through freewriting, revision, and peer response. These expressionistic influences appear in the text of her syllabus, where she tells students that they will do "lots of writing" and "learn to 'loosen up' and reduce some of our anxiety and fear around writing." However, in its emphasis on preparing for the WAT, the syllabus reveals the inherent contradiction in a course designed both to alleviate students' fears and to prepare them for a test that represents a barrier to their continued progress as college students.

In talking with Schnee, we learned that with some groups of students, she has confronted this contradiction directly by exploring current controversies in New York City over academic standards, bilingual education, the quality of high school preparation, and open admissions policies. In short, the current controversy revolves around whether the WAT test is really an accurate measure of students' writing abilities, especially for ESL students. The debate about the test went public when university trustees mandated that graduating students at Hostos Community College pass the WAT even if they had passed Hostos' own assessment test. When only 13 of the 104 graduating students passed the WAT, a heated debate began in the editorial pages of the *New York Times* and other New York City papers. For one assignment, Schnee gathered these articles and editorials representing a range of views on the issue. The headlines of these readings suggest the various arguments: "English Is an Art, Not a Science," "A Degree Devalued," "Victims in Workplace," and "CUNY Test Does Not Measure Writing Ability." She then asked students to write a response to one or more of the readings so that they could explore their own feelings and begin formulating arguments, according to the interview.

After extracting provocative excerpts from the students' writing and publishing them for the class, Schnee again asked them to write responses. The excerpts represented a range of opinions, with some students defending the WAT and others questioning its validity as a measure of writing ability. For example, an advocate of the test wrote, "Though I may agree that the test is flawed, I strongly support it . . . If you change the English requirements what will be next? . . . It really makes me wonder how these students passed in other subjects? Were they given special treatment because of the language barrier?" Another test supporter explained, "I don't want a devalued degree," while other students condemned the test: "I believe that the Writing Assessment Test (WAT) is a big farce." Another student saw the exam incident as symptomatic of a larger problem within the educational system: "The failure of the students at Hostos Community College . . . is a direct result of a crumbling school system." By prompting students to articulate a position on this controversy, Schnee encourages them to participate in this debate among "experts" that directly affects their college careers. She feels strongly that students should not be marginalized from this debate, and her assignments prompt students to define for themselves what a college education means and what a college-educated person should know. In confronting relevant issues with students, she complicates her expressionistic pedagogy and the skills development that prepares students for the WAT, inviting students to experience literacy not only as self-expressive and functional but also as critical and political.

By leaving space in the curriculum for the students' own agendas to emerge, Schnee practices an expressionistic version of critical pedagogy that stresses the need for students to engage with issues that impact their daily lives. For Schnee, when fully realized, critical literacy goes beyond self-expression, to thinking critically about an issue, and then acting upon that knowledge. She admits, however, that the action part is much more difficult for her to achieve in a workshop setting, especially when students are writing about intensely personal topics. If she can get students to see themselves as readers and writers—taking control of their own writing process—she feels she has introduced students to the first stages of critical literacy. As the students matriculate into the required writing courses, they can put these strategies into practice, Schee said in the July 21 interview.

First-Year Writing Courses

In addition to the basic writing workshops, Queens offers three credit-bearing, first-year composition courses: English 95 (for students who failed the CUNY WAT), English 110 (for students who have passed the WAT), and English 120 (an intermediate-level writing course). Chase and Murray teach these courses most frequently, and both instructors use a text titled *The Least You Should Know About English* to teach the basics of grammar, punctuation, spelling, and usage. While readings in Chase's courses tend to focus on the theme of work, Murray engages her students in a wide range of reading, including the daily newspaper, poetry, and works of fiction and nonfiction. They each described the need to teach to the WAT in English 95, but all their courses also emphasize "getting [students] interested in a reading and writing in a way that will carry beyond the test," Murray said in the interview on October 14, 1997.

In her courses, Murray wants students to see connections between reading and writing and to instill in them a desire to "become everyday readers and everyday writers." In the past, she has broken her 110 course into four sections—journalistic writing, poetry, fiction, and nonfiction—with the goal of exposing students to as many different kinds of reading and writing as possible. She tells students that people's reasons for writing vary from the purely pragmatic to "writing for the joy of it." One nonfiction text her students particularly like, Marjorie Shostak's (1981) *Nisa: The Life and Words of a !Kung Woman*, describes an interview of African woman from the Kalahari Desert. As Murray pointed out in the interview, her students often read about diverse cultures within New York, but have few opportunities to study cultures outside the United States.

Although Murray wants to preserve the cross-cultural aspect of her courses, she is currently rethinking her writing pedagogy. Through teaching in the Solidarity Project (see the next section), she learned the value of designing a course around a theme, discovering that "students are better writers when they know an issue deeply," which is difficult for them to do when a course covers so many different types of writing. Because the Solidarity Project involved "teaching students about the same issue from different angles," she felt that the courses developed their ability to write more complex arguments. Increasingly, Murray's pedagogy integrates both a literature-based approach and a more Freirean problem-posing, dialogical approach.

For English 95, Chase offers a "fairly traditional syllabus" designed to "improve students' essay writing and help get them through [the] Writing Assessment Test," according to a personal correspondence dated October 9, 1997. Along with the kinds of basic skills instruction Murray uses, Chase often brings in articles to give her courses a thematic angle, usually addressing a labor issue. Most recently, she designed an assignment around the issue of President Clinton's fast track legislation regarding the North American Free Trade Agreement (NAFTA). Class members first debated the issue with Muller serving as the judge, and when she ruled in favor of the union, class members realized they needed more information to make informed arguments on both sides. The class then read magazine and newspaper articles representing the differing points of views held by unions (described in the AFL-CIO publication *America at Work*) and big business (represented by a *New York Times* article describing Clinton's arguments for fast track legislation). To supplement their reading, students answered a series of questions Chase designed to help them understand the first article and "come up with more reasons and details to support [their] position[s]." For the second article, students designed their own questions for the class to answer. The assignment proceeded with students drafting an essay on the topic, participating in a second debate, and writing a final draft. With the WAT in mind, Chase works with students on their drafts to help them with correct punctuation, quotation, and citation of sources, according to the personal correspondence .

When teaching students grammar and usage in preparation for the test, Chase often includes lessons on diverse dialects. Since most of her Queens students speak Black English Vernacular (BEV), she addresses the issue of dialect head-on in courses, demonstrating the richness of BEV through readings by African American writers, especially Zora Neale Hurston, who move between what Chase calls "mass communication English" and BEV. Along with these readings, she also explains how the ability to switch dialects can be useful; for example when union leaders give speeches they often make use of "nonstandard" dialects that will be familiar to their members. Chase's approach to teaching language reflects Brookwood Labor College's emphasis on teaching and validating a "working-class vernacular" as part of their writing courses.

Solidarity Project

In Spring 1997, Chase coordinated the Solidarity Project, with the goal of "bridg[ing] two or three different communities" and "enhanc-[ing] understanding among different ethnic/racial groups."[6] The paired courses represent the culmination of a yearlong planning process that involved collaboration between Queens College Extension Center staff, faculty, and union leaders. The eight-credit course integrated "labor studies, writing, and a practicum in labor/community organization".[7]

In her final report for the New Visions Grant, Chase describes the Solidarity Project as a triangle: "those struggling with a social problem being one corner, the classroom being another corner, and the third corner being the student's project in her/his own community." The problem of sweatshops in the United States and around the world became the current social problem represented by the first leg of the triangle. Part of the course also focused on the Welfare Employment Program (WEP) and its effect on other salaried public workers. In the classroom, the triangle's second leg, students met in small groups to analyze the problem of working conditions in the garment industry, listen to guest speakers, plan their own field projects, and participate in peer response (faculty consulted with UNITE and CWA Local 1180 in designing the curriculum). The third leg of the triangle became students' field experience, in which they "[met] with faculty and union activists to plan out a campaign of solidarity with garment workers within their community organization, church, union, or in another context chosen by students."[8] Since most of the students in the class were African American and from the same public employee union, their collaboration with the garment workers, who are predominantly Asian American and Latino, created opportunities for cross-cultural understanding and solidarity. To create an intellectual base for their collaboration, students studied the issues surrounding the garment industry through Paul Mishler's Labor and Community Outreach course—the labor studies module—and gained practice writing about social issues in their social, political, economic, and historical contexts in Cara Murray's course in Newspaper and Article Writing—the writing module.

To link the labor studies and writing class, the students compiled a portfolio that faculty referred to as the Journal Project. As Mishler's syllabus explains, students made weekly journal entries about the class and readings (see Appendix D). Other assignments in the Journal Project included "writing projects for the Labor Studies and Writing modules, letters to the editor, newspaper articles written by the students, and reflective writing on the projects engaged in by the students."[9] While Murray periodically attended Mishler's class, the two teachers relied on the students' journals as a touchstone for their own collaboration. Through reading students' journals, the teachers could assess students' understanding of material, gain insight into students' thinking and writing, and keep in touch with the exchange of ideas going on in the other module. Through the Journal Project, the students' writing became the glue that bonded the writing and labor studies classes.

In the labor history module, which met on Saturdays from 9:30 A.M. to 12:15 P.M., students took a historical look at a labor movement by focusing on the garment industry in New York City, beginning with the late nineteenth century up to the present day. Faculty chose the garment industry because the Union of Needle trades, Industrial and Textile Employees (UNITE) campaign against sweatshops in New York provided a case study of a current social problem. Studying the garment industry opened up possibilities for student field experience since the UNITE campaign included a range of grassroots activities in which students could become involved (organizing workers, consumer boycotts, and public education). To gain a historical perspective on the UNITE campaign, students read extensively about union activism in the industry, ethnic politics, racism, and the impact of globalization. Writing assignments included informal responses to readings and speakers as well as a description of their UNITE practicum projects, which could involve writing fliers or union newspaper articles, making videos, giving testimonies before a hearing, conducting radio interviews, and presenting at work sites, union halls, churches, or community centers.

In the Newspaper and Article Writing module, according to the interview, Murray sought to help class members "extend writing beyond the classroom" and envision a wider audience than their teachers (see Appendix E). She wanted students to find a way to participate in public conversations about current issues affecting their lives. Because many students were already active in their unions, Murray wanted to teach them how reading and writing could enable them to accomplish their goals more effectively, perhaps through letters to the editor or writing articles for their union newspapers.

To teach students how to approach issues analytically before they take action, Murray had the class read cross-cultural articles and essays that analyze a social problem from different disciplinary perspectives. To demonstrate the process of cross-disciplinary analysis, Murray used a *Harpers* magazine article, "While You Were Sleeping." The essay describes a series of brutal rapes and killings that occurred in the border town of Juarez, Mexico. As Murray points out, the writer, Charles Bowden, rather than focusing on the killings themselves, places these atrocities "into the context of the global economy . . . symbolized by the maquiladoras, and their political, economic, historic, and social groundings." Murray supplemented this article with readings in economic theory, sociological texts calling the economic theory into question, and histories of Juarez and other border towns. These readings served as models for students' own writing projects, in which they identified an "issue which they believe[d] plagues our own social fabric" and discussed it in a larger economic, political, or social context.[10]

While most students chose issues related to the course theme (how sweatshops affect U.S. public workers), students who weren't union members chose alternative topics related to issues directly affecting them. One woman met with her young son and his friends to discuss "how, why, or if you should care about where your clothes come from, who made them, and how much [garment workers] are being paid." Another woman, an immigrant from Trinidad, perceived a wave of fear regarding recent changes in the immigration laws, including changes related to work requirements. After researching the changes through the Internet and getting the text translated into Spanish, she conducted an outreach project to educate people about how changes would affect them. A third student petitioned union leaders, through a letter-writing campaign, to take action on proposed changes in New York City's rent-control policies, arguing that this issue was of primary concern to working people. Murray and Mishler supported any student's topic as long as the project interested them and addressed significant labor issues, Murray explained in the interview.

While a number of students chose projects related to the issue of sweatshops in the garment industry, the secondary course theme of WEP workers received less attention in students' projects, perhaps because it became a source of controversy in the class. As Murray explained, students and teachers readily agreed that sweatshops represented unfair labor practices, and people were "ready to come to the aid of [exploited workers] not immediately in their own backyard." When discussing working conditions in Haiti, Mexico, or India, in Murray's view, students adopted "a bit of a patronizing attitude" that allowed the students to sympathize with workers in other countries who are only paid forty cents an hour. Since they felt little direct competition with these workers, the issue of sweatshops met with very little controversy in either course. Most students readily felt a sense of solidarity with the garment workers, making a project related to the UNITE campaign an attractive outcome for the courses. However, the issue of WEP turned out to be more controversial than either teacher expected because many of the students saw these nonunion, low-paid workers as threats to their own better-paid, unionized jobs, according to Murray.

In the WEP, welfare recipients receive training and work in public jobs for a paycheck, a process that would ideally lead to long-term employment outside the welfare system. Many unionized workers at the Queens Extension Center "knew WEP workers and saw them as the enemy. [They] had worked side by side with them and trained them and saw them as a threat to their jobs," acording to Murray. This attitude toward WEP workers posed an unexpected obstacle to their goal of using their courses to to create solidarity among workers. As Murray noted, they were "trying to make [student-workers] think beyond just scapegoating someone less fortunate than [themselves]" and help them "to develop a more encompassing understanding that if they fought against the WEP workers, they were actually fighting against themselves," according to the interview. Faced with a contradiction between their teachers' agenda and their own strongly held views, union members in the class tried to work through their thoughts and feelings in writing. Murray perceived their writing on the WEP issue as "more confused and contradictory . . . because it is an issue so close to them." Students struggled with the question of whether it was WEP workers or illegal immigrants who were responsible for taking their jobs away, while the instructors sought to redefine the question. According to Murray, both instructors argued their position strongly, hoping that "workers would see themselves as workers and not divide and conquer themselves by only seeing themselves as black workers or Latino work-

instructors response to controversial issues

ers and sort of making borders around themselves that would ultimately isolate them and throw them into corners so that they had no power at all." Perhaps because some of the city workers never saw the WEP issue the way their instructors did, when it came to choosing a final project, they either chose to get involved with the UNITE campaign or to focus on a separate labor issue of interest to them.

Teaching with a Political Agenda: An Activist-Radical Writing Pedagogy

The kind of activist critical literacy that threads through the Worker Education Program at Queens can be seen as a natural extension of a union-based program grounded in labor studies. All the faculty we spoke with at Queens share similar backgrounds either in union activism, labor studies, or radical politics. For them, the writing or labor studies classroom provides a space to enact the Freirean idea that teaching is a political act. Whenever possible, writing faculty at Queens practice what Shor refers to as critical-democratic education. That is, in their courses, they seek to guide students toward a critical consciousness regarding course themes, power relations, and societal values while at the same time helping students to succeed in the academic institutions that sometimes become the subject of their critiques.

Schnee's critical pedagogy seeks to empower basic writing students to see themselves as readers and writers who can use language as a tool for analyzing forms of oppression in their lives. In the workshop described above, she presents students with information about the controversy surrounding the WAT, giving them the opportunity to come to their own conclusions about the degree to which academic standards can legitimately be seen as oppressing certain groups of students. While students may not take action in response to their analysis, Schnee hopes they will understand the socially constructed nature of standards that may appear to students as "true" measures of their intelligence and abilities. Similarly, Chase's approach to teaching grammar emphasizes how what she calls the dialect of mass communication ("standard" English) gains its power not by its linguistic superiority over other dialects, but through its endorsement by the dominant class. Chase, Murray, and Schnee bring to their teaching an awareness that, for their working-class and minority students, standard definitions of correct and acceptable language use can work as oppressive forces as they seek to enter the academic world. To help students cope with this reality, these writing teachers offer strategies that enable students to perform linguistically as the standards require, but equally important, they diffuse the power of standards that define students as deficient.

In the Solidarity Project, the Extension Center faculty seeks to move beyond simply giving students the knowledge they need to cope with oppressive realities; they require that students translate knowledge into action. By choosing the campaign against sweatshops as a focus for the course, faculty gave students a real context for their writing and allowed them to experience the role of literacy in enacting social change. Rather than having students read about sweatshops in theory and develop plans for action from seats in an academic classroom, they gave students a chance to interact directly and meaningfully with a community group.

The Solidarity Project's focus on critiquing oppressive power relations raises the issue of internal consistency. As C. H. Knoblauch and L. Brannon argue, to be internally consistent critical pedagogies must hold themselves accountable for turning the same critical eye on their own liberal-radical ideologies and pedagogies that they turn upon dominant ideologies (1993, 163–69). In the Solidarity Project, curricular issues that critical-democratic educators might interrogate include how the course theme was selected, whether the theme allows for critical analysis from a range of opposing viewpoints, whether students can freely express views opposing the teachers' position, and how and when teachers offer their own viewpoints on the theme.

In reflecting on the two topics that were the focus of Murray and Mischler's joint classes—sweatshops and WEP workers, we see the WEP topic as a more effective theme for critical pedagogy. Because workers resisted Murray's position on the issue of WEP workers and had personal stakes in the controversy, the topic generated more conflict and thus more opportunity for examining the ideologies behind both the students' and the teachers' point of view. This sort of conflict seemed absent from classroom inquiry on the sweatshop theme because the issues seemed only remotely relevant to the students' immediate working lives. In addition, as it was framed, the sweatshop theme did not allow for a range of positions reasonable people could defend. Since this theme was so closely linked with the UNITE campaign, it provided an excellent opportunity for students to take action, but it left out a key element of an internally consistent critical-democratic pedagogy: a close examination of all relevant positions, including UNITE's policies, practices, and ideologies.

The WEP theme, in contrast, did generate substantial debate in the class, and because many students took positions opposing Murray's stance, the course raises the issue of what role the teacher's agenda should play in class discussion. Murray was surprised by her students' contrary position on WEP, and her students' resistance led her to rethink the goals of her activist-radical pedagogy. When one student in the Solidarity class published a letter to the editor in the *New York Times* that expressed a viewpoint that Murray "didn't completely agree with," she concluded that "in the end, it's just important for people to have a voice; you can't control what they're going to say with that voice or how they're going to use it. You can hope that they'll use it the way that you want them to use it, but the most important thing is that they use it," according to the October 14 interview.

Murray's willingness to reflect upon and rethink the goals of her activist-radical pedagogy characterizes the thoughtful approach faculty in the Worker Education Program at Queens bring to their writing instruction. In talking with Murray, Schnee, Chase, Muller, Sweeney, and Mantsios, we found them to be a group of educators committed to infusing their teaching with their political ideologies in self-reflective ways that engage working adults in dialogue about issues related to their academic and work lives. For them, however, dialogue alone is not enough. As Chase writes, "we believe that education is most effective when it couples reflection with action, and then that action is turned into further reflection."[11]

Notes

1. The center has a collection of essays entitled *A New Labor Movement for the New Century* (Monthly Review Press 1998).

2. Queens College, Office of Worker Education, *Proposal to Establish a Branch Campus and a New Bachelor of Science Degree in Applied Social Science to Be Offered Exclusively at That Branch Campus*, Spring 1997.

3. Quoted in an interim report for the 1996 CUNY New Visions Grant by Norah Chase, "Student Interdisciplinary and Community-Based Union Program," June 22, 1996, 1.

4. The Extension Center in Manhattan is currently directed by Sean Sweeny, who has been the director since 1995.

5. When the program began in 1984, the New York Joint Board of ACTWU provided a $225,000 endowment to support its members enrolled in college classes, according to the interview with Mantsios.

6. Norah Chase, "Final Report: Student Interdisciplinary and Community-Based Union Program" Planning Grant 1996, New Visions Program, CUNY Graduate Center, March 24, 1997, 1.

7. Paul Mischler, syllabus, "Labor Solidarity Semester," Labor Extension Center-Queens College, Spring, 1997, 1.

8. Chase, 1.

9. Mishler, 1.

10. Chase, 6–7.

11. Interim report for the 1996 CUNY New Visions Grant by Norah Chase, "Student Interdisciplinary and Community-Based Union Program," June 22, 1996, 2.

Chapter Six

Expressionistic and Critical Pedagogy
Swingshift College at Indiana University Northwest

I've always looked at education as a way of making people feel more confident about themselves, making people feel like what they do makes a difference and then getting people to the point where they want to make a difference and get involved.

—Ruth Needleman,
interview, October 9, 1997

In the early 1990s, when Ruth Needleman, the current coordinator of Swingshift College, worked as the education director for a service employees union, she first envisioned a college-credit program for adults that was "organically related to people's lives and unions," according to an interview on October 9, 1997. Inspired by the experience-based learning in Paulo Freire's worker schools in Brazil and by Highlander Folk School's approach to collective learning, Needleman's vision began to be realized in 1993 when she offered a one-credit course, Steel at the Crossroads through Indiana University Northwest (IUN) for workers at Bethlehem Steel. Beginning with this one course, she has built a program with steadily increasing enrollment that now serves approximately two hundred students, most of them steelworkers.

Now referred to as "Swingshift College," the program started with funds from a 1989 contract negotiation that provided workers in basic steel across the country with educational funds for noncredit and college-credit courses.[1] Like the Worker Education Program at Queens College, Swingshift College has a strong union affiliation, built through a cooperative effort between IUN, the Institute for Career Development (ICD), and the Local Joint Committees for Inland Steel, Bethlehem Steel, United States Steel, Republic Engineered Steel, LTV Steel, and Midwest Steel.[2] Students attending Swingshift College can earn either a certificate or an associate's degree in Labor Studies and General Studies at IUN. Like all IUN students, Swingshift students majoring in Labor Studies must take one semester-long writing course as part of their general education requirements (a second writing course is required for the Labor Studies associate's degree). Although the required writing course was recently offered through Swingshift for the second time, Swingshift faculty across the disciplines make writing instruction an integral part of any Swingshift course.

In talking with Needleman, Cathy Iovanella (instructional coordinator) and Doug Swartz (one of the writing instructors), we learned that a philosophy of writing instruction is still taking shape at Swingshift. Whereas Needleman has developed a strongly politicized critical pedagogy for her labor studies course—an approach that relies heavily on writing—in the composition courses, Swartz brings a less overtly political agenda and more expressionistic pedagogy to his Swingshift courses. Since this program is relatively new and still developing, the writing courses have yet to be significantly affected by Needleman's activist vision for the program. Yet like the other programs we have described, all the Swingshift course have been strongly influenced by the needs of the worker-students who participate in the program.

Adapting to Students' Needs

The mission statement for Swingshift College emphasizes—like Queens College—the importance of providing "college programs based on an appreciation for the unique life and work experience of each steel worker or adult learner" and "of offering relevant course to workers at convenient times and locations" (n.d.). The name "Swingshift" (coined by a student reporter for the Gary, Indiana *Post Tribune*) reflects the program's attempt to fulfill its mission through modeling class schedules after the work shifts of the steel mills. Each course is offered once a week and twice a day so that students can attend either the morning or evening class sessions, depending on their schedules. Since steelworkers often work twelve-hour or double shifts, some students must miss classes altogether, in which case videotapes and photocopied notes help them catch up on what they missed.

Other support services are available to students through onsite advisors, an instructional coordinator, and peer mentors called learning advocates or friends of their education/career development program. As the full-time instructional coordinator, Iovanella runs workshops on grammar, punctuation, and study skills in addition to serving as an in-class tutor, responsible for "troubleshooting," which begins with "looking for students who are uncomfortable or have problems," she said in an interview on June 13, 1997. Most important, she helps students make the transition from the factory to the classroom by developing relationships with students and, occasionally, resolving conflicts between students and faculty. Part of Iovanella's job entails consulting with the Learning Advocates, experienced Swingshift students who can earn up to six credits for serving as mentors, which includes taking customized courses such as Multicultural Communication and Leadership and Peer Mentoring. These courses prepare them for peer mentoring that might include anything from giving someone a ride to class to counseling peers about dealing with perceived barriers to going back to school. In courses for learning advocates, Needleman and other faculty provide training in interview techniques, and they encourage students to talk with classmates and coworkers to understand better their fears about going back to college. Students who become learning advocates seem to find the experience rewarding. As one experienced learning advocate, Gene Sufano, the first Swingshift student to complete a four-year degree, explained in a June 13, 1997, interview, he plans to "stay on as a peer advocate as long as [he is] employed at Inland Steel."

In talking with Sufano and other Swingshift College students who gave a presentation at the 1997 Working-Class Studies and the Future of Work Conference, we were struck by their sense of ownership in the program. They told stories about letter-writing campaigns to the administrators at IUN that helped bring about the growth of Swingshift and about their successful nomination of Needleman for a teaching award. As Kathi Wellington, a Swingshift student, explained in an interview on June 13, 1997, because students come out of unions, they have a strong sense that collective action can make difference. Her advice to an audience member at the conference who asked about starting her own program for worker-students was to "flood the dean with letters describing your situation." If you get no response, she continued, then tell the administration, "We'll go somewhere else if you can't meet our needs. We'll take our money elsewhere."

A similar spirit of empowerment permeates students' description of how they participate in hiring and evaluating faculty. As Sufano explained during the interview, "We put 'em through the ropes" by asking questions about what kinds of assignments and tests they give, and they ask them whether they "know what the working class is up against." He said they also "come right out and ask [teachers] how they feel about being videotaped." Once students deem a faculty member's pedagogy appropriate for Swingshift, learning advocates subsequently evaluate faculty at midterm and at the end of semester. In conducting the evaluations, the advocates talk with students about how the class is going before writing up their findings and meeting with the professor to share the results. In one evaluation, for example, some students objected to a professor's lecture style because they wanted more interaction. As Iovanella and Needleman helped the learning advocates and the professor understand, a lecture style that works on campus may not translate to Swingshift, where students expect interaction and enjoy voicing their opinions. While some faculty may be uncomfortable during these critiques, Iovanella explained in the interview that professors usually take them seriously when they revise courses for future classes.

An additional way students exert influence over the curriculum is through membership on the Curriculum Committee of the Swingshift Advisory Board. By serving on this board, students have a voice in what courses are offered, often reminding faculty of courses that need to be offered for students to complete their programs. Students also help customize Swingshift courses to reflect their interests. Students typically will meet with instructors before a class begins to review and negotiate requirements, readings, and assignments. In part because of students' input, faculty who teach at Swingshift tend to build into their assignments frequent opportunities for revision, along with flexible attendance and late-paper policies. As Needleman pointed out in the interview, Swingshift seeks to adapt curricula to students' needs and to cultivate a love of learning by creating courses that make learning fun and relevant to students' lives. This course description for a macroeconomics course illustrates the elements of "fun" and relevancy in Swingshift courses:

> *Guns* and *Butter, Diamonds* and *Water*, the *Grasshopper and the Ant,* and Baby *"Bonzonomics."* Doesn't that sound better than *"Monetary Policy and Its Effect on Inflation?"* You already know economics! You practice economic principles every day, and you may have been the victim of them. So why don't you join us and learn some "real world" macroeconomics. If nothing else, you might learn a foreign language . . . *econospeak!* (fall course flyer, 1997)

While this macroecomics class was adapted to appeal to worker-students and unionists, it still focuses on the same goals as the on-campus version of the course. Sometimes courses are packaged differently so their titles indicate more clearly how the course might be relevant to working adults or to adapt to a thirteen-week, three-hour class session format.

While these courses include legitimate academic goals and college-level work, the subject matter embraces broad issues and topics often offered through noncredit, continuing education programs. The curriculum reflects a more practical approach to education than we saw at Whitehead or Queens, where the "host" universities saw themselves as selective institutions that could not afford to be "stigmatized" by offering what might appear to be a separate kind of "adult education." As Needleman explained, the administration of IUN—after convincing on her part and successful pilot courses—now accepts that the "steelworkers have bought this program"; that is, the program exists for two reasons: one, because the student-workers take courses for free (they are paid for out of an ICD customized course fund) and two, because the steelworker-students and career development coordinators from the mills have been willing to work with Needleman to develop the program, according to the interview. The university's trust in Needleman's judgement, combined with continual input from the students, the union, and mill coordinators, has allowed Swingshift College to mix more traditional academic courses in English, labor studies, and economics with a series of one-credit, nontraditional, customized courses on topics such as Drug Testing in Workplace, Workplace Sexual Harassment, and Coping with Aging. These one-credit courses might be seen as "bridge" courses designed to attract students' interest and get them involved in more in-depth university study (they can sign up without being admitted to the university, taking placement exams, or submitting transcripts).

Writing in the Labor Studies Curriculum

The idea of giving students a bridge to academia also underlies Needleman's approach to teaching labor studies.[3] To engage students in the subject matter, she uses "fun, interactive, and practical" writing assignments, according to the October 9 interview. She and other labor studies instructors select texts that students find compelling (such as Staughton Lynd's *Rank and File* and Bridgid O'Farrell and Joyce L. Kornbluh's *Rocking the Boat*) and use them as springboards for interview-based personal writing assignments, for example about their family's history of work and their own unions, said Iovanella in the interview on June 13, 1997. According to Swartz in an October 3, 1997 interview, students find Needleman an inspiring teacher and mentor. He observed that "they give her a lot of credit for the program, for their own intellectual development, and their own willingness to take chances . . . She convinces them that they won't fail, that they'll get whatever help they need, that the program will accommodate anything that comes up."

Students' respect and appreciation for Needleman's work grows out of her constant efforts to design creative courses that employ engaging assignments that provoke thoughtful discussion and writing. In the first labor studies course Needleman designed for Swingshift, Steel at the Crossroads (a five-week-long, one-credit course), she introduced students to a variety of readings and videos on labor history, took them on a field trip to a Japanese-managed steel plant, and brought in guest speakers on technology issues. A writing assignment for this course asked students to draw upon readings, the tour, and their experience to reflect upon how they would have done things differently if they had been president of Bethlehem Steel during the 1980s when massive steel mill closings took place. For Needleman, this assignment exemplifies her goal of combining creative, fun writing with serious thought about issues of decision making and the impact of technology. A related assignment began with students drawing two pictures of their department, one five years ago and one today, as a basis for writing about the effects of technology on the workplace, the union, and workers' skill levels. The excitement this course generated in workers, who gained insight into changes they had experienced in their workplaces, led Needleman to create a customized one-credit course called New Technology in the Workplace.

The element of creativity in Needleman's writing assignments helps students feel comfortable at Swingshift, but she also brings to her courses a serious political agenda: to enable workers to gain control over their lives and become agents of change. She seeks to educate steelworkers about the history of their industry and unions from a pro-labor perspective, thus creating a feeling of continuity between union workers of the past and present. Moreover, Needleman designs courses and assignments that encourage students to use their academic knowledge to take action through writing editorials and articles for newspapers and the union newsletter. For the History of Steelworkers course, Needleman invited to class many "pioneer" steelworkers, "men in their eighties and nineties who had helped build the union," including a participant in a legendary steel strike that took place in 1919. This event and the video "The River Ran Red," about a major strike in Homestead, Pennsylvania, led to a writing assignment comparing the working conditions of steelworkers in the 1890s and 1980s. For this assignment, Needleman had a specific pro-labor agenda—to demonstrate to current steelworker-students, who may not be well versed in the long history of steelworkers' activism, that "you can't blame workers' apathy for declining unions when workers and unions are being crushed," according to the interview. At the end of the class, students translated their learning into action by filling the Christmas issue of their union newspaper with articles about what they had learned in the course. As Needleman pointed out, these articles not only educated other workers about union history and allowed students to apply their learning, they also provided good publicity for the program.

Writing assignments play a central role in Needleman's activist teaching because she is extremely self-reflective about her own writing processes and has strong empathy for the struggle composition poses for any writer. When Swingshift first began, she argued for waiving the writing placement exam, recognizing that, especially for adult students, the test might evoke anxiety and fear of failure based on memories of past school experiences.[4] Realizing that returning students would need extra help with writing, she originally hoped to have a writing tutor in every class. While this goal never materialized, she was able to hire Iovanella, who offers writing workshops and tutoring for first-year required writing courses and courses across the curriculum. Whenever students feel they need one-to-one work on their writing, they can turn to her for extra help.

In Needleman's own classes, in addition to designing challenging and creative writing assignments, she offers liberal revision policies, focuses on content more than grammar, and discusses with students her own struggles with writing. She believes that students learn best from writing and rewriting, explaining that even experienced writers like herself usually throw away their first three drafts. Through emphasizing revision and drafting, she teaches them that good final written products cannot result from "writing off the top of your head." It is through writing, she tells students, that you "figure out what you have to say." Needleman's belief in the value of revision has led her to consider requiring students to rewrite some of their past labor studies essays that they thought of as "finished." Though she is not familiar with the literature on revision in the field of composition studies, she intuitively understands its importance based on her own experiences with writing.

Similarly, while Needleman has not read the extensive research pointing to the value of collaborative writing, her belief in collective action and building community leads logically to her growing interest in using collaborative writing assignments. She sees herself as "an organizer-educator not an educator-academic," and she especially enjoys working with groups of people affiliated with a single organization. Her experience in union education and a trip to Freire's worker education schools in Brazil taught her that "if you could get a group of people together and work with them, they would go back together and transform their organizations." In the context of Swingshift, Needleman believes such transformative action becomes possible when the steelworkers, most of them belonging to the same union organization, feel a sense of community and solidarity within their college classes. She sees writing as a way to build relationships within a classroom, and her goal is to encourage more "collective learning and writing" in all Swingshift courses, from peer response to co-authored assignments. Increasing students' opportunities to write collaboratively advances her "hidden agenda" of building the kind of solidarity that leads to effective union activism.

First-Year Writing Courses

Doug Swartz, who taught the two first-year writing courses that have been offered to date at Swingshift, takes a less political approach to his teaching than Needleman, but they share a desire to help students feel more confident in their writing. Both teachers seek to create a supportive community in the classroom, where worker-students' past life experiences are highly valued and deemed relevant to their academic work. Swartz believes strongly that Swingshift students, whether they realize it or not, are already writers who have fairly extensive experience. To show students the writing strengths they already have, Swartz praises them for improvements from draft to draft, comparing them favorably to student drafts he receives for on-campus courses. He tells them that the course is designed to "accredit them for what they do and have already done," although the course will also help them with some basic strategies for academic writing, especially "using the library and applying their interests and experience in an academic context," according to the interview.

Trained as a Renaissance scholar, Swartz became interested in teaching writing at Swingshift when he heard other faculty describe it as "exhilarating to teach returning adults who have so much to say and are so committed." Teaching in a program for working-class union members also appealed to him on a political level. He laughingly described himself as "a kind of callow academic leftist with no real political engagements to speak of," and for him, teaching at Swingshift "sounded like one way to get involved with some people that [he] sympathized with." As a professor from a middle-class background, Swartz initially didn't want to presume that he knew anything about teaching adults from working-class backgrounds, and although he describes himself as interested in working for the kinds of (pro-labor) social change Needleman supports, he also felt ill-equipped to use his teaching to help enact change "with any sort of credibility or integrity."

Instead of developing an activist pedagogy similar to Needleman's, in his first Swingshift courses, Swartz took what we categorize as an expressionistic approach to teaching writing by encouraging students to see themselves as capable writers who already possess the creativity and ability necessary to write well. He encourages students to use expressive discourse as they become familiar with conventions of academic forms such as the research paper. He sees his role as bridging real and perceived gaps between students' working worlds and academia. He explained in the interview that students "have felt excluded from the university or they excluded themselves from it a long time ago." As a result, they imagine a considerable gap between their union work and reading for pleasure and what is required in college classes. Swartz sees his part of his job as "just saying it's pretty much the same thing, you just have to translate from one to the other."

To ease students into academic work, Swartz uses what he described as an "ad hoc" approach to composition instruction. That is, he offers a loosely structured curriculum in which students freely choose their own writing topics and work through revisions of their texts through small group peer response, individual conferences, whole-class discussion of sample student writing, and self-reflective essays for their portfolios. In the first writing course, students wrote page-long journal entries and longer papers, both on topics of their choice, to be submitted for a grade at the end of the course in a portfolio. Swartz believes students' choices of topics should depend in part upon their reasons for taking college courses: Students who are seeking degrees in a particular discipline may want to use the class to become familiar with academic forms of writing, whereas students taking courses primarily for self-fulfillment may prefer to undertake what Swartz sees as more nonacademic assignments such as writing family or union histories, according to the interview.

Swartz's ad hoc approach, which focuses on helping students set and meet their own goals for their education, complements the Swingshift philosophy that students should participate actively in decisions about pedagogy and course design. In the interview he said he sees his role as "drawing people out and letting them establish the curriculum." As many Swingshift teachers do, Swartz met with the students before the writing courses, and together they decided to use Jeff Sommers and Cynthia Lewiecke-Wilson's *From Community to College*. Instead of working through the text's assignments and readings in a linear fashion, the class read essays that represented different styles and genres of writing, from journalistic to academic. Using these examples and the text's assignment prompts as a guide, Swartz helped students generate topic ideas by making lists of writing they had done and might want to do. Rather than giving specific assignments, Swartz encouraged class members to write about whatever interested them, explaining that he would give them feedback on their writing at any point in the semester, but that the only grade they would receive would be for their final portfolio.

Swartz's delayed approach to grading and the latitude he gave students for choosing their own writing assignments unsettled some students, who felt they needed more structure (i.e., clearer directions, firmer deadlines, and more feedback in the form of a grade). As Iovanella explained, many Swingshift students are "overachievers" and see grades as an important measurement of their progress, so Swartz's approach of having no set due dates, no formal assignments, and no midterm grades created some confusion and frustration. The dissatisfied students didn't communicate with Swartz directly but instead talked with Iovanella and the Learning Advocates, who often mediate between students and faculty. Before offering the course for the second time, Swartz talked with students who had taken the first course, new students, and Iovanella, agreeing to fine-tune his course by giving students a midterm grade on a rough-draft portfolio, more direction in their journal writing assignments, and firmer due dates. This kind of negotiating between students and faculty is not unusual at Swingshift. Needleman, Swingshift faculty, and Iovanella encourage students to take control of their learning experience and to communicate their needs and concerns to the teacher or the learning advocates. As Swartz commented, it is students' willingness to voice their opinions about their classes that makes teaching at Swingshift exciting and challenging.

While some students felt uneasy with Swartz's flexible approach to teaching writing, most of the students we talked with described Swartz's class as a positive learning experience. One woman explained in an interview on June 13, 1997, that she left the class feeling more confident as a writer because of Swartz's portfolio approach: "At the end, you had yourself a nice little portfolio, which everybody was real proud of. It was the first time in my lifetime I ever had a portfolio. . . . it was a step-by-step process, one step after another, building one after the other. I think everybody gained confidence." By focusing on "what's strong and worth working on" in students' portfolios, Swartz is able to accomplish his goal of showing students that they possess the strong linguistic abilities that form the basis for effective college writing, according to the interview on October 3, 1997.

Just as Swartz has a strong respect for students' language abilities, he also values students' working-class histories and experiences and sees his students as educating him about their work in the steel mills and about union culture. For example, when several students wrote grievances for one of their writing assignments, he explained, "students wound up teaching me how write these things." They knew that you had to "make the language forceful enough but vague enough so that you get what you want but they can't say that's all that you get. It was a very intriguing glimpse into a form of rhetoric that I could talk about that way, but they just knew it from experience," he said.

At times, readings for the class formed a bridge between students'
knowledge of working-class culture and Swartz's knowledge of academic culture. The class read sample essays in *From Community to College*
on sexual harassment in a paper mill and environmental issues a
painter confronted on his job. Other readings did not focus on work or
working-class life because Swartz believes readings should not exclusively relate to students' experiences. He "doesn't want to assume that
students only want to read working-class literature" because they also
express strong interests in other kinds of literature such as world literature. However, through readings that do represent working-class life,
Swartz did provide openings for discussion and writing about students'
own workplace-related issues and experiences. For example, one student wrote about how her mother's struggle as a working-class woman
is representative of working-class life in general. Another student un-
covered a chapter in history by telling the story of Mexican Americans
who were deported from steel mills in the 1930s. Like the sample essays from the course text, these students' essays draw upon personal
experiences as a basis for experimenting with different genres of writing, including the kind of research-based academic writing that Swartz
introduces them to in the course, according to the interview.

In spring semester of 1998, having taught two first-year writing
courses at Swingshift, Swartz team-taught an intermediate writing
course with Robin Hass. The course focused on different forms of
working-class writing, and Swartz met with students to solicit ideas for
texts and assignments (see Appendix F for a sample assignment). Because many of the students are working class, Swartz felt that designing a course around working-class literature would be appropriate. In
addition to offering writing courses at the intermediate level that immerse students in texts relevant to their disciplines, Swartz also sees a
need for initiating discussions among faculty about writing across the
curriculum. Since faculty in labor studies and sociology, for example,
teach and expect a lot of writing, he hopes they can work together to
develop a common style sheet. He also envisions developing a Swingshift writing center to supplement the support students already receive
from Iovanella and Learning Advocates.

Expressionistic and Radical Writing
Instruction at Swingshift

The writing courses we analyzed at Swingshift College seem cross-
pollinated by Swartz's expressionistic pedagogy and Needleman's commitment to creating courses across the curriculum that take students'
working-class history and experience as the starting point for writing

and discussion. Needleman's commitment to activism as a goal of education, along with students' own activist agendas, seem likely to influence further the teaching of writing at Swingshift. Since Needleman and the students take such an active role in course development, we foresee Swartz's expressionistic pedagogy shifting toward a more social-critical approach to teaching writing. With the new writing course on working-class literature, for example, Swartz's pedagogy will almost inevitably begin to incorporate the kind of economic, political, and social critique that is often missing from expressionistic rhetoric (Berlin 1988).

At the same time, because of Swartz's self-reflective stance toward teaching writing and his reluctance to overtly politicize his classroom, he seems likely to approach any shift toward a social-critical pedagogy cautiously and thoughtfully. Moreover, because curricular and pedagogical choices at Swingshift are never top down, students will almost certainly have input into any significant changes. Because Needleman and her staff actively seek dialogue that takes students' voices seriously, Swingshift College seems to be moving toward Gerald Graff's vision of a university where students have a voice in debates between advocates of "traditional pedagogy, critical pedagogy, feminist pedagogies and various other pedagogies" (Buffington and Moneyhun 1997, 7). At Swingshift, students are not in the disempowering position of moving from classes where "the rules suddenly change without notice, and the only way the student can cope is to give the teachers what he or she 'wants'" (7). Rather, students have a voice in making the rules.

As Swingshift's mission statement points out, "Swingshift College is unique; the program is not 'owned' by one institution but is a cooperative effort between [Indiana University Northwest, United Steelworkers of America, the Institute for Career Development], and the students."[5] More than any program we studied, Swingshift College provides an educational site where students have the opportunity to act as equal participants in a whole range of decision making—from hiring and evaluating faculty to choosing course texts. Just as Brookwood Labor College students did, Swingshift students regularly question teachers' pedagogies and challenge institutional norms. Swingshift College itself exists, in part, because students demanded that administrators and faculty envision a new, innovative mode for delivering education to working adults.

Notes

1. Swingshift College is not an official college but a program established at IUN, with its own separate mission statement and advisory board that includes

IUN administrators, faculty and staff, ICD coordinators, the career development coordinators from each participating steel mill, USWA representatives, and Swingshift students.

2. The ICD was created to oversee the educational funds negotiated in the 1989 contract.

3. Needleman is one of several labor studies teachers in the program.

4. When Swartz began teaching writing in the program, he negotiated with Needleman to have students take a writing placement exam that could be administered in a nonthreatening way. He felt the exam would be extremely useful in understanding the different levels of writing ability people brought to the classes, Swartz said in the interview on October 3, 1997. The placement exam is given before students take a course, and no one is screened out on the basis of the test.

5. Quoted in an unpublished report written by Iovanella, 1997.

Chapter Seven

Teaching on "Turns"
Youngstown State University's
Writing Courses for Working Adults

No matter what jobs I have held over the years, I have reserved a place in my mind for this reemergence into the academic world. I guess I still needed to prove to myself that it was a viable option and that I still had the ability to succeed at the college level.
—Denise Sigler,
interview, October 4, 1995

In a down-at-its-heels part of town, past a used car lot, at the end of a long driveway, the steelworkers union hall building looks like a run-down military barracks, sandwiched between deserted buildings and struggling family-owned businesses. Inside, the attic has been converted to a comfortable learning space, where students move between classrooms with seminar tables, a modern computer lab, and a small reading library. This location has been the site of a series of Youngstown State University (YSU) writing, literature, labor studies, and math courses designed specifically for full-time steelworkers.

As a result of the same national contract that jump-started Swing-shift College, in September of 1994, the Steelworkers Local 1375 approached YSU about offering a program consisting of onsite courses leading to an associate's degree in Business or Labor Studies. The steelworkers union found a business curriculum attractive because they

believed a business degree would offer its members job opportunities in
the event of a mill closing or if workers' jobs were phased out because
advanced technology made them "redundant." University administrators responded positively to the idea, viewing it as one strategy to com-
bat dwindling enrollment and as a means to serve adult learners in the
surrounding working-class communities.

To allow students to meet requirements for the degree, the first
union hall courses offered included a labor history course and a writing course that would meet general education requirements. Before the
courses could be developed faculty and administrators worked with
union officials to solve the problem of making the courses accessible to
steelworker-students, who work on a system of twenty-one "turns," in
which workers rotate weekly between day, afternoon, and night shifts.
Using Swingshift College as a model, the university agreed to offer the
same course twice a day at the union hall so that students could attend
a morning or afternoon class depending on their shift that week. This
system called for an unusual sort of team-teaching in which two faculty members shared the same students and used similar classroom activities, but one faculty member taught in the morning, the other in the
afternoon.

In the fall of 1994, John Russo, who had taught labor studies
courses at the union hall in the past, invited Strom to teach the first
writing course because of her interest in working-class studies. To plan
the course, Strom consulted with Belanger, with whom she had team-
taught courses in the past. For the second course, the two of us became
coteachers, and we subsequently designed a series of college-credit
writing courses for working adults at the union hall. The courses, which
explored the theme of work from historical, philosophical, and sociological perspectives, reflect our evolving application of critical pedagogy
to writing courses for working adults.

Teaching Writing in "The Little Red Schoolhouse"

When we taught the first writing courses at the union hall, our colleagues referred to the program as "the little red schoolhouse" because
the courses combined students whose placement scores indicated a wide
range of writing abilities. Jan Kotwis, the Institute of Career Development learning coordinator, shared the concern of Ruth Needleman of
Swingshift College that tracking the steelworkers-students based on
placement scores would make some students feel stigmatized and less
confident in their ability to succeed in college-level courses. Because
teaching a course with students from mixed placement levels dovetailed
with our belief that collaboration among students with different kinds

of abilities can benefit both experienced and less-experienced writers, we readily agreed to teach a mixed-placement course. We felt mixing placement levels made sense considering that all the students felt anxious about taking a college-level writing course; one outcome of the mixed placement was a feeling of solidarity among students that expressed itself in a willingness to help one another.

Having combined students who had placed into "basic" writing and those who tested into the regular first-year course, we designed a curriculum that would allow us to teach the stated goals of the on-campus writing program while adapting those goals for this unique teaching situation. The on-campus sequence of four writing courses (two of them designated "basic") progressively moves students toward the goal of writing a researched argumentative essay that represents a kind of generic academic discourse (i.e., the writer is expected to consider various points of view, use sources responsibly, support points with relevant evidence, and use edited Standard English). Rather than teaching three or four separate courses, we synthesized the goals of all four courses into one class that used a workshop format. While all students practiced writing personal narrative and research-based essays, we developed separate evaluation criteria for students at each placement level, expecting more extended arguments and better control of style and punctuation from the more advanced students.

To create a student-centered classroom culture in which students could develop confidence in themselves as thinkers and writers, we began each of our writing courses by helping students explore their ideas about the purposes of writing and what they wanted or expected to learn in a college writing course. Each course began with individual conferences in which students set their own writing goals for the quarter. Typically, items on students' lists included general writing goals such as improving spelling and punctuation while other writing goals focused on students' desire to take transformative actions: to write better grievances, help children with homework, or write convincing letters to the editor. Rather than simply imposing standard course goals on students, we sought to establish from the beginning that students' own concerns and ideas would be integral to the course. Periodically, students wrote self-evaluations to reflect upon their progress toward their initial goals and to record their developing ideas about effective reading and writing processes. These self-evaluations built students' confidence in part because they celebrated successes, but also because they gave students a sense of control over their learning process. These texts allowed follow-up discussions with students to be dialogic negotiations that balanced students' own perceptions of their progress with standard course goals and teachers' expectations for particular assignments. This process of negotiation and self-reflection established mutual trust between students and teachers, laying a foundation for collaborative peer response and small-group discussion that made up the daily activities of the classes.

The Theme of Work in a First-Year Writing Course

As part of the student-centered environment we sought to create, we put working-class history and experience at the center of our writing curricula. To validate working-class culture and experience, we chose the theme of work for the first two writing courses. Students in the first class taught by Strom read selections from Robert Sessions and Jack Wortman's (1992) *Working in America: A Humanities Reader,* which focuses on the philosophy, history, and future of work. The readings gave students a larger context for analyzing their work experiences, which have been shaped by the decline of the community's once thriving steel industry.

In Strom's first writing assignment, a personal work history, students wrote about the shift from stable to unstable employment, documenting the numerous shutdowns, layoffs, and strikes that characterized many of their working histories. Juxtaposing their work experiences with the discussion of work in the assigned readings, they used their personal experiences to critique readings that approached the subject of work from an academic perspective—an approach they found privileged and naive. Perhaps because they saw themselves as authorities on the topic of work, they felt entitled from the beginning to question the authority of published texts, even when the level of academic discourse felt unfamiliar and intimidating. Because the ideas in readings interested students, rather than giving up when challenged, they regularly read assigned essays three or four times without prompting. In one class, for instance, after students' first reading of Frihjof Bergmann's (1992) "The Future of Work," they initially reacted in anger, arguing that the author wrote an essay that used too many big words and expressed the ideas indirectly. With dictionary in hand, they read the essay a second time, looking up unfamiliar words and identifying ideas they could understand. Reading the essay a third time, they began to engage fully with the ideas and some students even developed an appreciation for Bergmann's style. This process took place outside the classroom, with students reporting back to Strom during the class' first discussion of the essay. By the time they came to class, students had already described their reading process in a journal response, and they were eager to discuss the essay. While not all students reacted the same—that is, some still felt uncomfortable with Bergmann's style— they all persevered in reading the essay at least three times.

Using Bergmann's ideas as a starting point, the students formulated their own theories about how work at the steel mill and in the community could be restructured to provide meaningful employment for more people. Of all the essays read that term, Bergmann's essay elicited the most interest and excitement as it led students to express their feelings about work in general, fears about their jobs being eliminated by technology, or concerns about a mill closing in the near future. In response to class discussions and a Labor Day editorial in the local newspaper, one student wrote an essay titled "Labors' Pains" and published it in the union newsletter. The students' strong identification with the issues raised by the theme of work gave many of them confidence in their ability to express their points of view in writing. Their developing facility with written language provided a solid base for the next course, in which they would be asked to write an extended researched essay that, for many of them, would also count as a final project in their labor studies course.

Writing History: Pairing Labor Studies and First-Year Composition

In the second union hall writing course, taught in winter 1995, Belanger joined Strom, who had taught both "shifts" of the first course. Together, they collaborated with Russo, who was teaching a swing-shifted labor history course. Because many of Russo's students were also enrolled in our writing course, the three us had an exciting opportunity to collaborate across disciplines and create links between our courses. The collaboration seemed natural because of our shared belief in creating curricula that validate working-class culture and experience. Russo approaches the teaching of labor history "from below"; that is, rather than emphasizing major strikes and great labor leaders, he focuses on helping students to chart the everyday histories of working-class people. In his winter 1995 courses, he taught the students to generate research questions that would allow them to construct working-class histories of their communities, becoming active constructors of knowledge rather than passive recipients of experts' versions of history. The eight- to ten-page essays resulting from this research represented a culmination of what students learned in Russo's labor history class and our writing course.

In the writing course, we complemented the labor history course by assigning a historical labor novel, Thomas Bell's (1976) *Out of This Furnace,* and several historical-sociological essays about life in early twentieth century steel towns.[1] These readings and short writing assignments prepared students for the longer research project. We began by reading and writing journal entries in response to *Out of This Furnace,* an account of immigrant steelworkers' experiences in early twentieth-century Pittsburgh. Through students' journal entries, we found that this text validated their work lives even more directly than the previous course's readings. For example, one student's response to reading the first section of the novel outlines various ways in which "the life in the steel industry one hundred years ago was similar in many ways to today's steel mills," particularly in terms of workers' attitudes toward management and feelings about working shifts. The main difference, he notes, is an economic one; he points out that, unlike current workers, those in the novel "worked hard, long hours and still lived in poverty." However, as another student points out, the fact that "many steelworkers today have felt the agony of being one paycheck away from poverty gave him an 'eerie feeling' when reading the novel." These strong feelings of identification were experienced by all the students. Most important, however, this text, with its detailed explanation of work in the mill, its use of language and customs associated with the Slavic culture, and its geographical locale all contributed to turning the tables in the classroom: As we mispronounced names of characters, puzzled over detailed descriptions of blast furnace operation, and struggled to imagine where communities mentioned in the book could be found in modern-day Pittsburgh, we relied on students' cultural knowledge of the mills, the Slavic community, and the Pittsburgh area.

While we began the course encouraging students to draw upon their cultural knowledge and see themselves as expert readers of *Out of This Furnace*, we asked students to build upon that framework of knowledge by engaging in critical dialogue with several chapters from an academic book written by sociologist Margaret Byington, *Homestead: The Households of a Mill Town* (1969). Her chapters on working and living conditions in turn-of-the-century mill towns deal with many of the same social and political issues that arose in the novel, but differences in the two sources demanded that students evaluate the competing versions of truth represented by their readings of the novel, Byington's essays, and their experiences. In their writing, students grappled with issues of meaning while learning to follow conventions for writing academic essays. Out of this struggle and through research in the labor history class, students generated their own original research projects.

While we worked with students on reading and writing strategies, Russo divided his two-day-a-week course into two sections: One day he lectured on working-class people's contributions to labor history; the other day he ran a research workshop. In these workshops, students might, for example, formulate ideas for their projects, getting input not only from Russo but from their classmates. The benefits of having students brainstorm as a group as their research projects took shape is apparent in the story of how two labor history students' projects became interconnected. The idea for the first student's project emerged when Rex Raub found at his grandfather's house a book of 1920s photographs of Truscon Steel Corporation, the forerunner of Republic Steel. The photographs' visual power opened up for Raub a moment in which the past and present coalesced, producing a sense of timelessness. He saw in the photographs evidence of both continuity and change: Some machines looked the same as ones currently in use, while others had been replaced. When Raub brought the book to class, Russo encouraged him to consider the photographs as a critical primary source, one that might potentially help to fill in gaps in the written historical accounts of the steel industry. It was not, though, until some of the other students began examining the photos that some of their most significant contents came to light. Denise Sigler, through her project, had sought to discover the earliest presence of women in the mills; until she looked at the photographs, she had had no sources of information revealing their employment in steel mills during the 1920s. Interviews with nursing home residents provided some information, but in looking at the photographs, she noticed women dressed in crisp uniforms and working in the tin mill, a finding that gave her the same personal sense of continuity with the past that Raub had experienced.

This sense of a real connection with the past often became the starting point for students' writing projects, all of which relied upon research techniques described in Jeremy Brecher's (1988) *History from Below* rather than on more traditional library sources. These techniques include transcribing oral histories obtained through interviewing and analyzing videos or photographs documenting the building of local unions. This community-based research was particularly appropriate for the union hall classes because it allowed students—many of whom had unsuccessful experiences with reading and writing in high school —to engage in academic projects that legitimized ideas and experiences from a familiar working-class culture.

To celebrate students' accomplishments in the course and to provide a real audience for their work, we organized a reception at the end of the term at the Youngstown Museum of Labor and Industry. Students invited family and friends, and we invited union officials, university administrators, company management, and university faculty. The more than one hundred people who attended browsed through displays of students' projects, which included photographs, tapes of interviews, videos, slide shows, and artwork. By actually talking with these readers of their work, answering their questions and receiving praise, students' sense of themselves as true experts on their topics and as "real" writers was reinforced.

Case Study of a Steel Strike: A First-Year Writing Course

A writing course in the fall of 1995 began just as our students' union went on strike; coincidentally, we had decided to develop the course's reading and writing assignments around the Little Steel Strike of 1937, a strike against Republic Steel plants in Chicago, Youngstown, and

Warren, Ohio, which is where our students' union hall is located. Since many of our students' fathers and other family members worked at Republic Steel as both rank and file and as managers, they brought a collective memory of this violent conflict to the class. For our students and for the Warren community, the strike of 1995 became a kind of palimpsest of the 1937 strike, with rhetoric, key players, and artifacts of the earlier conflict resurfacing to imbue the current situation with the spirit of the past.

In the weeks preceding the 1995 strike, our students read accounts accompanied by original photographs of the '37 strike in the current issue of *The Warren Steelworker,* the union's newsletter. In an issue featuring articles on the '37 strike, newsletter editor and union president Dennis Brubaker's editorial entreated the current union membership to prepare themselves for a possible lockout or strike if the upcoming negotiations broke down (1995, 2). Then, just two months before the 1995 strike (and three months before our class began), the Ohio Historical Society hosted a colloquium that brought together members of the Steelworkers Organizing Committee (SWOC, the precursor of the United Steelworkers of America), a local journalist who covered the action, and community members indirectly affected by the strike. The colloquium served to publicly create an oral history of the "climactic and often violent 'Little Steel' Strike of 1937" (Brubaker 1995, 1). Many of the organizers—including the strike captain and Communist leader Gus Hall, now eighty-five-years-old—returned to the Youngstown-Warren area, and, through their reminiscences, reawakened in community members and in many Local 1375 steelworkers the legacy of activism that galvanized the strikers in 1937. The public oral history they created was framed by an account of the strike presented by a labor history student and a labor historian. This event, by interweaving "expert" academic opinion with "history from below," reinscribed the pedagogical approach students experienced in the writing and labor studies classes, in which students conducted original research based on interviews, analyses of original documents in the archives of the Youngstown Museum of Labor and Industry, and experts' conflicting representations of history.[2]

Just as the '95 strike went into full swing, the fall quarter writing courses, centered around the strike of '37, began. Students sandwiched their course work between shifts on the picket line, and our classes were moved from room to room to make space for meetings, food distribution, and child care. For the first assignment, students wrote about what they knew and felt about the current or past strikes. Through the assignment, we gained insights into how the few students in the class who were not steelworkers felt about labor and management issues. As one of these students, eighteen-year-old Amanda Lather, wrote, she felt "nervous about taking the class at the union hall with so many older students" (class journal, 1995). She was also "worried that she didn't know enough about unions to take the class"—her only experience with them was walking past people holding picket signs outside a local nonunion grocery store. The assignment also encouraged students to express their prejudices, biases, assumptions, and emotional reactions. One steelworker-student vented his anger at the company for hiring replacement workers:

> When we were first locked out and I realized that there were replacement workers, hundreds of them, in the plant, I became very angry at the company . . . the goons were a symbol of the company's willingness to use brute force if necessary to ride out the first storm until they could get an injunction that would permit semi-civilized disorder. . . . That first 48 hours many thoughts streaked in and out of my temporarily shell-shocked mind. As I joined my brothers and sisters on the picket line and at the union hall, it soon became apparent that there was hope from many individuals that this would be a work stoppage of short duration and things would return to normal. This false hope scared me. The company was successful at everything they attempted, and to think that they would be unsuccessful suggested diminished rationalization based on hopes for a favorable outcome to this confrontation. (class journal, 1995)

This assignment helped students see writing as a means of self-expression and laid the groundwork for future exercises involving rhetorical analysis and critical thinking.

To give students tools for this type of analysis, the class worked through a series of applications from Vincent Ryan Ruggiero's (1995) text *Beyond Feelings: A Guide to Critical Thinking*. We chose this text because we wanted a brief rhetoric that could be easily applied to our "case study" of the strike, and the text was on our department's list of approved course texts. Because *Beyond Feelings* acknowledges the important role intuitions and emotions play in critical thinking while also exploring their limitations, it seemed especially appropriate as a guide to analyzing the highly charged, emotional situations of the past and present strikes. The text's applications ask students to use their own experiences to examine the concepts of objectivity and subjectivity through exploring the questions of what constitutes truth, knowledge, and a "sound" opinion.

A typical early assignment invited students to explore social and cultural factors that affected their identities and beliefs by answering the question "Who am I?" in ten different ways, then exploring which self-descriptions are most important to them and why.[3] Through discussing such an assignment in groups, students began to see how factors such as race, age, class, and gender shape how they see and are perceived by

the world. One woman, who worked for an automobile parts manufac-
turer, described the impact of being raised in a primarily male environment (she'd "rather have a dirt bike than a diamond ring") where her
mother was a "typical dependent housewife" (Cheryl Ross, 1995). Her
list prompted her to analyze ways she consciously sought to emulate
what she saw as the positive masculine role models and eschew the
"negative" feminine one by seeking technical work, a managerial position, self-sufficiency, and independence. As she began developing her
own research project later in the course, we encouraged her to explore
possible connections between her upbringing, her identity, and the
anti-union positions she took in later writing assignment.

While some students had an easier time seeing such connections,
the goal of the assignment was to help students identify where their
opinions came from and how reading, writing, and thinking processes
are affected by socially constructed beliefs and values. As one student
explains in his midterm self-evaluation, the applications led him to see
that responses to issues are filtered through individuals' experiences
and biases: "There are many factors that control the outcome of your
response. Issues that may seem clear-cut to you may be less black and
white to others. Initial reaction to a topic may keep you from seeing
both sides. You might only favor views that support yours, and discredit
all others" (Dan Leihgeber, 1995).

After practice applying critical strategies to situations in their personal lives, students' next assignment was to analyze the public, published discourse surrounding the 1937 strike. First, the students read
conflicting versions of the strike by David Brody (1987), labor historian
and author of "The Origins of Modern Steel Unionism"; Gus Hall
(1987), the strike captain and author of *Working Class USA: The Power
and the Movement;* and Tom Girdler (1943), the company president of
Republic Steel and author of *Bootstraps.* For each reading assignment,
we asked students to use the critical thinking strategies developed in the
first assignments to analyze and evaluate the truth value of the varying
accounts. In journal entries recording their first readings of each text,
students tended to summarize material and had difficulty doing the
kind of careful analysis that would move them beyond their personal
viewpoints, often shaped by the degree to which they felt allegiances to
the union. This excerpt from a student's response to Gus Hall's book is
one of the most problematically uncritical of the student responses:

> In this article there were a lot of good points about Communism. Gus
> Hall was a very courageous person. I think in the beginning he could
> foresee what was going to happen . . . I think the Communist Party
> cared about the workers. I think Gus Hall should be looked up to for
> the factory workers' rights of today. Where would we be without him?
> (Anna Maldanado, class journal, 1995)

After reading students' initial responses, we asked the class to reread the texts, this time imagining what Gus Hall might say in response to Girdler's account of the strike, how Girdler might respond to Hall, and what Brody might say about each of their accounts. We also asked that they review earlier assignments on evaluating the truth value of an argument. Subsequent class discussions pushed students' thinking—for example, they began to question Girdler's assertion that his climb through the ranks of the steel industry made him an "insider" who could understand the concerns of working people better than "outside agitators" such as Hall. Numerous students also interrogated Hall's self-representation as the hero of the strike:

> Gus Hall's tribute was very biased toward the greatness of Gus Hall. The author was willing to downgrade anyone it could to make Gus Hall look superior. Very strong unsubstantiated claims were made in this writing, especially saying in effect that Ronald Reagan appointed criminals to the White House. Gus Hall was wanted on warrants in six different states, yet the author never explains each warrant directly, you are only led to believe that each of them was false. (Dan Leihgeber, 1995)

Similarly, students began to see how the Brody article could be read as intervening in this debate by putting Girdler's and Hall's accounts of the strike in a larger framework, one in which neither of the two men were even mentioned by name.

Along with giving students a framework in which to reread Hall and Girdler, the Brody piece challenged students to decipher its academic language and immerse themselves in a discourse community into which students unfamiliar with the history of steelworkers' organizing efforts had difficulty entering. In the morning shift of the class, often attended by traditional YSU students and workers in other industries, the students struggled to make even literal meaning of the text. Whereas key terms and players in the historical events were unfamiliar to the morning students, steelworkers-students in the afternoon shift of the class took over the teaching of that text, explaining ideas such as the difference between an open and closed shop and the significance of the Wagner Act. Through this experience, the steelworkers, teachers, and other class members collectively constructed a foundation of knowledge for rereading all three texts in order to prepare for the first major writing assignment.

The first multidraft essay assignment placed students in a fictitious, rhetorical situation calling upon them to analyze the three sources we read as a class and then evaluate the texts' arguments for a specific audience. In one option, students wrote to a friend interested in researching the "SWOC years"; for a second option, students prepared the text for a talk for a colloquium on the SWOC years much like the one recently held at the Youngstown Museum of Labor and Industry. Both options required that students draw upon the readings in *Beyond Feelings* as well as their own experiences in considering the kinds of evidence and arguments used by the authors. In addition, students reflected on how their own biases had led them to "read" this moment in history in a particular way. This challenging assignment required that students generate criteria with which to evaluate their sources, apply the criteria, and then adapt and organize their analysis for an audience.

In our experience, a multifaceted assignment like this one often meets with some confusion and resistance in first-year students, both on campus and at the union hall site. We find students often struggle when asked to "read against the grain" as David Bartholomae and Anthony Petrosky describe it: to question a writer's arguments, examples, or vision; to engage in a dialogue with the text (1986, 10–12). In a June 20, 1996, interview, student Anna Maldanado laughingly reflects back upon her early naive readings of the opposing accounts of the '37 strike by Hall and Girdler: One text "was management and one was the workers. . . . first [we read] Gus Hall and we hated management, and after reading the CEO, my opinion changed completely and I hated Gus Hall." Another possible explanation for the difficulties students such as Maldanado experienced early in the course is that inexperienced college writers have not been exposed to a wide range of written discourse patterns required of academic writers. The complex reading and writing assignments in this course gave students experience with a variety of the discourse options available to writers, which as Mike Rose notes, are "essential to the making and conveying of meaning in our culture" (1987, 331). Meanwhile, the applications in *Beyond Feelings* provided a kind of balance: They validated students' abilities as sophisticated thinkers by helping them discover ways in which they were already using these same interpretive and evaluative strategies to discover meanings in their everyday lives.

In midterm analyses of their work, many students commented on what they had learned from the SWOC assignment. Leihgeber, for example, wrote that "researching different sources was good to do because I usually try to rush my process and sometimes do not find the time to read different sources. The way this class is structured forced me to take the time to read different sources and see the biases that occur in writing" (class journal, 1995). While some students struggled to organize and present their analyses, many students—as Leihgeber's comment suggests—attained through this assignment a richer understanding of how critical analysis can make them more self-reflective and better able to consider and evaluate different points of view.

Midway through the course, students' abilities to respond thoughtfully and reasonably to an opposing viewpoint were put to the test when Cheryl Ross—a nonsteelworker in a management training position—wrote an essay that critiqued the union's actions during the 1937 strike. On the day Ross presented her draft to the class, she was nervous that her point of view would not be well received or respected. The discussion that followed was lively but not hostile, focusing on the effectiveness of her argument; many of the students concluded that they found her ideas persuasive and challenging, but disagreed with her conclusion. Significantly for this student, this experience reinforced the idea that even potentially hostile audiences can be receptive to an opposing argument if the writer makes her case by fairly presenting opposing points of view and openly acknowledging her own biases. The draft she presented to the class gave a balanced view of her topic, conceding, on the one hand, that "the 1930s was a time in history [memorable because of] the contributions of the CIO, SWOC and the dedicated men and women who fought to shape the future environment for the working-class people" while still asserting that "it is also important to take into account that the companies also had a valid position for their stand against the unions." In the end, though many of her classmates disagreed with her thesis, they appreciated that this balanced approach effectively supported her main claim that union organizers of the 1930s used objectionable means to achieve their goals.

In her midterm self-evaluation, "Writing Behind the Scenes," Ross wrote:

> Writing is more than having a pen and pencil in hand. It involves critical thinking, interpretation of the ideas of others, and being able to formulate a theory leaving some of our personal biases behind.
>
> Critical thinking is the topic that has hit me the hardest. Everyone is quick to say that they are a critical thinker. The [steel company] employees feel the union is a necessary stronghold and are quick to defend it, right or wrong. Yet, I found myself in my initial draft taking the other stand and jumping down the union's throat. A day or two later when I read it again, the bias of my writing was alarming. I too had fallen victim to my environment and beliefs. (1995)

This student's process of making an informed argument, presenting it to a knowledgeable audience, and then reevaluating her position in light of her own biases demonstrates well many of the strategies that empower students with the knowledge and critical tools necessary to be effective members of their union, workplace, and community.

By the end of the course, as students began work on their research projects, they also began commenting on their growing appreciation for the importance of language. Through the reading and writing

assignments that required students to analyze the main conflicts between management and the union in the 1937 strike, they had gained
valuable experience in analyzing competing versions of truth. As student Barry Frommelt pointed out in his portfolio self-evaluation, this
type of analysis made him aware that language is not neutral and that
carefully crafted words can have powerful effects in the world: "Nothing put-to-paper crossed my eyes without some study as to how, who,
why, thought this was the best way to express their ideas. Sometimes,
this process became more interesting than the written text" (1995). We
are convinced that students' process of reaching this kind of insight, a
worthy goal of any writing course, was facilitated by the unique relevance and immediacy of their learning context—the union hall setting
in the middle of a strike—and the content of course—the rhetorical
situation of the 1937 strike. Based on our experience in teaching this
course, we see creating and building upon such learning contexts as an
important element of the most effective literacy education.

Reflections on Our Evolving Pedagogy

After teaching the first three union hall courses, we began considering
various theoretical frameworks that might help us characterize our approach to teaching working adults. In Nicholas Coles and Susan V.
Wall's 1987 essay for *College English,* a social approach to teaching basic
writing to adults employs some of the same strategies for teaching academic discourse that we use. Coles and Wall's description of their process for introducing students to university discourse represents an approach we initially felt comfortable using, but as we analyzed their
approach more closely, we found ourselves reflecting increasingly on
the relationship between students' and teachers' ideologies in the classroom and how these ideologies affect the teaching and learning of
literacy.

The issue of ideology emerges in the Coles and Wall piece when
they argue throughout the text that students' writing in response to the
theme of work is often "politically simplistic" because it is informed by
the "ethos of individualism with its faith that hard work and a good
education guarantee economic success" (1987, 310). In the article,
Coles and Wall give no indication of whether they discuss with students
the differing ideology they as teachers bring to the classroom. They
seem to depend on readings—such as Studs Terkel's *Working* and Richard Wright's *American Hunger*—to challenge what they see as students'
naive ideologies. Their comments suggest an important measure of
good reading and writing is the degree to which students become
proficient readers of both the text itself and the teacher's implicit polit-

ical goals for the course (e.g., to critique the culture's dominant ideology of success). We recognized in Coles and Wall some of our own pedagogical blind spots—in particular not having thought through when or how to foreground our ideologies and open them to question.

While our students often write about political issues and we sometimes require them to do so, we had not fully examined any ideologies we bring to our teaching. Nor were we certain which of our beliefs and values should be openly acknowledged in class and laid out for students to analyze and critique. We found one model for foregrounding and critiquing ideology in the writing class in the work of Donald Lazere (1992b), who advocates that teachers openly discuss their own ideologies and pedagogies at the beginning of a course. Lazere's rhetorical approach to analyzing competing ideologies embedded in political rhetoric prompted us to articulate how our own ideologies might be shaping our classroom practices. With discussion between the two of us most often focusing on our mutual commitment to developing effective student-centered pedagogies, we had avoided serious discussion of ideological differences that might be affecting our classroom practices.

One topic we knew we approached from somewhat different perspectives was unionism. Strom brought a strong pro-union bias to her teaching based on her knowledge of union's past history of improving working conditions for the laboring class. Because of her prounion stance, she often encouraged students to write about unionism or union history. This bias is evident in our choice of the 1937 Little Steel Strike as a case study topic for the course. Compared to Strom, Belanger brought to the union hall courses a more skeptical stance toward unionism. Because Strom took a strong pro-union stance, to balance that perspective, Belanger wanted to make sure management's perspective was represented in readings and class discussion. We realized that had we been teaching the course separately, we might not have been as aware of how our own ideological biases were shaping reading and writing assignments. However, even though the dialogues we had while planning the course helped balance our biases, we realize now that the class setting—a union hall—and our students—mostly union members on strike— influenced both of us once the class began to be less critical of pro-labor rhetoric than we might have been in another classroom context.

As we look back on the course we taught using the 1937 Little Steel Strike as a theme for writing, we realize that although we asked students to begin the course by identifying their personal biases and knowledge about strikes and labor issues, we never overtly shared our own ideologies with the class. Had we done so—and maybe even shared some of the dialogues that took place as we designed the course—we could have opened our own course design and assignments to students' scrutiny.

An interesting assignment might have been to ask students to analyze the rhetoric of our assignments, looking for signs of our ideological biases. We could have posed the question of how a union hall setting and the classroom context of a strike affected our perceptions of how language was used in the 1937 conflict. If we had spent more time teasing out the ideologies all of us brought to the course theme, it might have created a more open classroom, where both teachers and students could interrogate one another's interpretations of the rhetorical strategies employed by participants in the 1937 conflict.

We see our writing pedagogy evolving toward a fusion of Lazere's frontloading of teachers' ideologies and his emphasis on rhetorical analysis with Freire's concept of transformative action. In addition to giving students practice in analyzing rhetorical strategies in other people's discourse, we believe that an empowering literacy involves using language to enact change in the world. As the previous chapters have illustrated, writing assignments that lead to social or community action have a long history in union-based programs for working adults. In our courses for steelworkers, we stopped short of incorporating writing assignments in which students could apply their new awareness of language to an actual rhetorical situation. In retrospect, we see the union hall as what C.H. Knoblauch and Lil Brannon call an "oppositional site"; that is, a space sanctioned by the academy but grounded in the surrounding community that provides opportunities for meaningful action not always feasible in more traditional academic settings. This kind of space allows teachers to take risks and experiment with pedagogies in collaboration with adult students, many of whom bring to the classroom strong investment in work and community issues that gives them an impetus for action.

Notes

1. We would like to acknowledge Nancy Moore of the Community College of Allegheny for recommending readings by Thomas Bell and Margaret Byington and several related writing assignments.

2. Of course, we remind students that participants' testimony in oral histories can be just as conflicting (or even as inaccurate) as traditional approaches to labor history and business unionism Nevertheless, Brecher's *History from Below* provides a methodological framework that promotes the development of basic and historical research skills and the strengthening of participatory and community unionism.

3. This exercise comes from Vincent Ryan Ruggiero (1995), *Beyond Feelings: A Guide to Critical Thinking.*

Conclusion

In "Collegiate Life: An Obituary," Arthur Levine and Jeanette S. Cureton (1998) describe a shift in expectations for higher education as both traditional and nontraditional students increasingly view college as just one of many activities in their busy lives. While traditional students still enjoy some aspects of campus life, "they're doing what's necessary to fulfill degree requirements and gain skills for a job, but then they're out the door" (16). This utilitarian approach to higher education is also evident in working adults' growing demand for high-quality, low-cost education delivered at convenient times and locations. As Levine and Cureton point out, both on-campus and commuting students approach education as consumers of a product, "believ[ing] that since they are paying for their education faculty should give them the education they want" (14).

As working adults exercise their ability to choose from a number of educational "products," colleges and universities find themselves competing with new stripped-down degree programs that "offer low-cost instruction made possible by heavy faculty teaching loads, mostly part-time faculties, limited selections of majors, and few electives" (14–15). Faculty and administrators find themselves faced with the challenge of maintaining the integrity of traditional degree programs while adapting delivery modes and curricula to the needs of working adults.

The five programs we studied have already developed strategies for offering adult students flexible delivery modes and relevant, rigorous curricula. In their writing programs, we found faculty dedicated to providing working adults with courses informed by contemporary composition theory. In each case, the program's theoretical perspective was shaped by the larger institutional context. Union-based programs tended to gravitate toward Freirean writing pedagogies that emphasize literacy as a means to reflective social action. Their pedagogies most directly reflect the radical roots of education for working adults in the labor colleges of the 1920s and '30s. Corporate-identified programs teach a less radical form of critical literacy, emphasizing mastery of discourses that will lead to reflective participation and success in academia and business. Their emphasis on upward mobility and self-improvement is reminiscent of the drive for knowledge and economic success that fueled nineteenth-century mechanics institutes and lyceums.

Despite their differing ideologies, what unites the union-based and corporate-identified writing programs we studied in the past and present is their vision of writing at the center of learning. In these programs, first-year writing courses (or their equivalent) are often just the beginning of an ongoing process of writing instruction that extends into courses across the curriculum. Beginning with Brookwood Labor College, we discovered a rich history of cross-disciplinary faculty in adult-oriented programs using writing as the cornerstone of their pedagogies. Though the details of past courses are yet to be fully explored, we find similar kinds of interdisciplinary, writing-intensive courses in today's programs: At Whitehead College, students write experiential learning essays that incorporate cross-disciplinary knowledge to analyze past learning experiences; in the Queens Extension Center's Solidarity Project, faculty pair a history course with a news article-writing course; at YSU, we pair labor history courses with literature and composition courses. Faculty at Swingshift College, Empire State College, and Whitehead College described examples of how they used writing-to-learn activities to teach content material in classes such as business, social work, psychology, labor history, and literature.

Beyond individual classes, faculty in every program expressed interest in expanding their present efforts to incorporate writing in all their courses or studies. Faculty seemed to recognize readily the opportunity writing gives students to explore a topic deeply through multiple disciplinary lenses. Because the faculty we interviewed were strongly student- and writing-centered, they were enthusiastic about the possibility of cross-disciplinary conversations about writing that would involve both students and faculty. Building a strong writing across the curriculum program dovetails with participatory classroom practices often valued by faculty in adult programs such as collaborative learning and dialogic discussions. Therefore, the process of extending writing instruction beyond first-year courses and across the curriculum promises to be a smooth transition in programs for adults.

We see placing writing instruction at the center of education for working adults as a key to designing effective writing curricula within the context of alternative delivery modes, especially if writing pedagogies focus on critical literacy. Convinced by Freire's strong case for connecting literacy and action, we see action-oriented writing pedagogies as valuable because such approaches treat knowledge and literacy not as static entities but as dynamic tools for meaningful personal and social change. In fact, we see transformative action as a vital extension of participatory writing instruction even when students' plans for action conflict with ideologies of the teacher or institution. Although students and teachers may disagree about what constitutes a meaningful or appropriate action, this sort of disagreement would not necessarily signal the failure of the critical process. We believe that an internally consistent critical pedagogy leaves space for the possibility that the teacher's own ideology might be naive or insufficiently interrogated. As long as teachers guide students through a collaborative process of reflecting critically on both teachers' and students' ideologies, we advocate developing action-oriented pedagogies suited for the flexible yet rigorous degree programs sought by many working adults.

As we have shown, educators in this country have been adapting curricula, pedagogy, and delivery modes for adult students since the early nineteenth century. Evening lectures, night courses, informal study circles, and weeklong seminars characterized early modes of delivering education to workers through lyceums, mechanics institutes, Socialist Party study circles, women's clubs, union-sponsored Unity Centers, community colleges, and union-university programs. For working adults, these institutions and informal groups provided a viable alternative to more traditional forms of higher education originally designed for eighteen-year-old, white, privileged, male students. Current programs continue this tradition of creative, flexible delivery methods by offering courses that will be accessible to adults working full time in or outside the home. Through decentralized off-campus courses held at convenient times, accelerated courses, and distance education, all the institutions in this study have found ways to create "universities without walls" that are "unbound by time and place."[1]

Of all the programs we studied, we see Empire's move toward offering more on-line writing courses as the most predictive of where education for working adults is headed in this technological age. As U.S. workers log in more hours on the job, leaving less time for leisure and education, distance learning promises a time-efficient way for highly motivated adult learners to earn college credits. With businesses and union halls gaining access to the Internet, the demand for on-line education can only grow (see Appendix G for a description of an off-campus YSU course for working adults that incorporated some elements of distance learning).

When programs begin adapting their delivery methods to the needs of working adults, they often adjust institutional policies to make their programs more adult-friendly. In the labor and two-year colleges, open admission and affordable tuition gave access to worker-students who because of either lack of appropriate credentials or sufficient tuition money could not have attended traditional colleges or universities. At the labor colleges, adult students didn't face obstacles such as placement tests that often led them to be tracked into stigmatized remedial courses at the community colleges. Instead, they took classes with fellow workers with a range of educational backgrounds and writing abilities. Because the goal of past programs was to provide a nurturing but challenging space for adults to pursue their education, institutional policies—like delivery methods—remained necessarily flexible.

Current programs also find detours around potentially constrictive or restrictive institutional requirements through creating separate admission policies, developing alternatives to placement exams, and providing off-campus services from advising to textbook sales. In the case of selective institutions such as Whitehead College and Queens College Extension Center, they established separate criteria for evaluating applications from adult students. By using work experience and minimal age requirements as criteria for admission, these two colleges acknowledge the special circumstances of returning adult students. At Swingshift College and YSU, both of which are open admission, placement polices pose a larger obstacle to adults. Through mixed-ability writing classes, both programs have reduced the anxiety and stigma often associated with placement tests and tracking. Conversely, the recent CUNY decision to require all students to pass mathematics, reading, and writing placement tests before admission will pose a serious threat to programs like the Queen's Worker Education Program. Because such programs see their educational role as providing a scaffold for adult students who seek to enter the university, rigid admission requirements risk excluding highly motivated, capable students for whom traditional predicators of success in college may not be relevant.

With increasing numbers of students combining work and study, fewer and fewer students are well served by a traditional model of higher education that assumes a student body of eighteen-year-olds able to devote four to five years of uninterrupted study on a college campus away from work and family. Faculty and administrators in this study represent educational pioneers who through their foresight refashioned delivery modes, curricula, and pedagogies to meet the needs of working students. Through their innovations, they have created a well-marked path to guide other colleges and universities into the educational landscape of the future.

Note

1. The phrase "university without walls" is the name of Skidmore College's distance education program; the second phrase comes from Empire State Center for Distance Learning's Web page.

Appendix A

Program: Alfred North Whitehead College
Instructor: Staff
Course: Experiential Learning Portfolio
Topic: Interpreting Experience (model syllabus)
Date: Fall 1997

Catalogue Description of LSHU 310: Interpreting Experience

Students interpret their experience and that of others to develop written, oral, and critical thinking skills. Integral to the process is creation of a portfolio of experiential learning that can be evaluated for additional college-level credit. Attention is paid to interpretation of experience through biography, autobiography, and literature.

Course Description

Interpreting Experience is composed of six class sessions, each of six hours duration, and is delivered over a twelve-week period. Students will learn the differences between describing and interpreting experience and why those differences matter in the context of college, the workplace, and general learning. Students will examine the effects of role, contexts, and words upon interpretation as they examine diverse ways of interpreting experience.

The course investigates critical approaches and applies them to texts and personal experiences. Students will start by examining a variety of articles and literature (visual arts also may be utilized). Through this critical examination, students will gain an appreciation of the role of perspective in the interpretation of experience. Students start by writing their autobiography, the foundation of their portfolios of experiential learning, and progress to the writing of essays that challenge courses in the University of Redlands catalogue. Students are also expected to incorporate into their essays theoretical and conceptual learning in such a way as to demonstrate college-level learning. The course aims to strengthen writing skills and foster the development of critical thinking skills.

Course Objectives

As a result of satisfactorily completing this course, students will

- learn to reflect critically upon their own experience and that of others
- through portfolio-development, bring the process of documented self-evaluation into clearer focus
- create a document that may be submitted and evaluated for additional academic credit, if additional credit is needed for degree completion
- improve their ability to analyze, synthesize, and evaluate textual material in an increasingly complex manner
- learn how to evaluate the work of peers in the shared review of experiential learning essays
- improve thinking, writing, and oral communication skills

Texts and Resources

Bartholomae, D., and Petrosky, A., eds. 1996. *Ways of Reading: An Anthology for Writers*. 4th ed. Boston: Bedford Books of St. Martins.

Bateson, M. C. 1996. *Composing a Life*. New York: Penguin Books.

Feiler, B. 1991. *Learning to Bow*. New York: Ticknor & Fields.

Kubler-Ross, E. 1969. *On Death and Dying*. New York: Macmillan Publishing.

Portfolio Guide. 1996. Redlands, CA: University of Redlands.

The writing handbook currently being used in the major program will also be used as a resource.

Filmography

The Color Purple	*Rashomon*	*Ballad of Little Jo*
French Lieutenant's Woman	*Lone Star*	*Shadowlands*

Course Topics

- creating an experiential learning portfolio
- writing an autobiography
- using the ANWC experiential learning model

- brainstorming, mindmapping, and mining the information
- reading a text critically
- interpreting experience in conjunction with theory
- researching
- exploring diversity

Appendix B

Program: FORUM (Empire State College)
Instructor: Elaine Handley
Course: Group Study
Topic: Our Working Lives: Writing for Meaning
Date: Spring/Summer 1997

Purpose

Writing is a connective process—it helps us find meaning in how we live and what we do while living. We spend a huge portion of our lives making a living—engaged in work that will keep us afloat economically, help us develop useful skills, provide ourselves with an identity and sense of purpose, and give us an opportunity to interact and build relationships outside the family structure. In Studs Terkel's words, "it is about a search . . . for daily meaning as well as daily bread, for recognition as well as cash, for astonishment rather than torpor."

In this study, we will look deeply and critically into our notions of *work*. Most of us work for hire, but we work beyond our employment. Our hobbies, our support of causes, our relationships with partners, children, and parents are also commonly acknowledged as work. We also refer to our concerns with our individual self as "working on myself." John Gordon, the author of "More Than a Job," writes: "These dynamics of personal experience, social relations, hope and disillusionment are what make work so interesting, so complex, so ambiguous and contradictory, so many things at once." In this study, we will write for meaning on as many aspects of work as possible, and hopefully we will discover in what ways the different aspects of our work hold meaning for us.

Activities

In this study, we will read a variety of texts that should provoke you to reflect, think critically, and begin to write analytically about your own and our culture's definition of work. We will also explore concepts related to work such as "time," "avocation," "calling," "professionalism," and "self-esteem" to name a few. You will write six short papers (students are encouraged to experiment with form and voice) and at the third residency submit a portfolio of writing, including a final summary paper that will provide you with an opportunity to reflect on what insights you've gained in this study through your writing, reading, and class discussions at residencies.

Texts

Autry, James. *Life and Work: A Manager's Search for Meaning.* Avon Books.

Charters, Ann, and Samuel Charters, eds. 1997. *Literature and Its Writers: An Introduction to Fiction, Poetry, and Drama.* Bedford Books.

Rechtschaffen, Stephan. 1996. *Timeshifting: Creating More Time to Enjoy Your Life.* Bantam Doubleday.

Terkel, Studs. 1974. "Introduction." In *Working.* Pantheon.

Walker, Alice. 1983. *In Search of Our Mother's Gardens.* Harcourt Brace Jovanovich.

Although this is a primarily a writing study, the readings were carefully chosen. They are meant to provoke your thinking, your memories, your aspirations. They offer different perspectives on a variety of issues having to do with work. Your reaction to the reading will become part of your journal writing, and perhaps part of your writing assignments. The reading assignments will be an important jumping off place for our residency discussions.

In *Life and Work,* James Autry's writing will serve as a model for your own writing in this study. Autry was a successful Fortune 500 executive who discovered that writing was a way for him to integrate his life and work. Much of his writing is about management. In an interview he said: "It [business] doesn't exist without people, whether they are the customers or the vendors or the employers or the investors. It is an enterprise of humanity, and the manager's role deals precisely with that . . . if I can manage the people well—create the environment in which they can grow and feel fulfilled and be part of this new neighborhood, and friends as the new family, which is called the job—then they will themselves almost indemnify me against some of the mistakes I might make on the technical side."

In *Literature and Its Writers*, we will read poetry, short stories, and a play. There are many ways to write about the work issues, and writers have done so in different genres since the beginning of time. In this study you are invited to experiment with different forms and different points of view for your writing assignments. You can write a poem, a short story, a screen play, or a personal essay for any of your assignments. You might try writing one of your assignments from the perspective and voice of a coworker, your boss, your spouse, your child, or someone who reports to you. You are encouraged to experiment in this study—to use your imagination, as well as your brain and your heart.

Timeshifting is a book that argues a point of view. You're asked to look at the text as an argument to see how effectively the writer defends his perspective. This book was also chosen because of the compelling points it makes about time. For many of us in midlife we think of time as our nemesis, an entity we cannot control. Rechtschaffen argues that time is a tool, which aware or not, we use to shape the quality of our lives—and our attitude and use of time is what affects our working lives.

Work Journal

As a way to record thoughts and ideas for writing assignments you will keep a work journal. The work journal will be the tool you use to observe your own work habits and attitudes about work—as well as those you interact with. Each week you are to write a total of four hand-written pages. You may decide if you want to keep a daily journal, a once-a-week summary, or some other rendition. Writing in your journal regularly will not only help you establish a rhythm of writing, but it will also sharpen your observation skills. It's essential that you write in your journal no less than once a week. You may keep your journal on a disk and hand in a hard copy. If you choose to keep a journal by hand, choose a notebook that is easy to carry with you and write in. The more accessible it is, the more likely you are to write in it.

Your journal observations will be provoked by the reading assignments, memories, current experiences, stories, daydreams, night dreams, relationships—anything related to the concept of work. Your journal should become both a record of your thoughts and feelings about work, but also a place where you can first identify ideas for your papers. Attached to this learning contract are a list of issues having to do with work. Each week choose one these issues to write about in your journal. At least one page of your journal writing per week should record your reaction to the reading assignment for that week. The reading may help you choose which issue to write about, or your writing might be a result of some experience you've had at work. Please write what the issue is you're writing about at the top of your journal entry and be sure to date each entry. You will hand in your work journals at each residency, and your journal will be returned to you within a few days. Please note that your work journal is highly informal—it will not be judged on proper mechanics or spelling—it will be read only as a record of your thinking.

Portfolio

The final assignment is for you to assemble a portfolio of your writing. The purpose of the portfolio is to pull together your best writing and thinking on the subject of work. In the portfolio you may include revisions of any of the six writing assignments you've written for the study; you may also include any journal entries you think are appropriate. You must include a final summary paper that describes the insights you've gained about your working life as a result of the study's reading, writing, and discussions. It may help you to think of the portfolio as a written collection of your observations and feelings about work that you might hand on to someone in the next generation.

Appendix C

Program:　　Empire State College
Mentor:　　Sue Oaks
Course:　　Educational Planning
Topic:　　Learning Inventory and Learning Portrait Essay
Date:　　1996

Question: What Do I Know/ Not Know/Want to Know?

Assignments:

- learning portrait essay
- prior college-level learning assessment, as appropriate

The process of self-assessment always starts with a focus on you as a learner—the skills and knowledge that you have, the areas in which you are interested, the values that have caused you to develop those interests and skills. So it's important to start the process of self-assessment by reflecting on and identifying your current skills and knowledge.

The exercises in this section—a skills/knowledge inventory, an interests inventory, values identification, and an inventory of past learning experiences—are designed to help you think reflectively about yourself as a learner. Please do them fully and thoughtfully. They will help you complete the required "learning portrait" essay assignment at the end of this section. Also it may be important to share these inventories with your advisor, so he/she can get a fuller picture of your skills and knowledge.

What Do I Know/Not Know?

The skills/knowledge inventory, the first exercise that you will be asked to do, should be thought of in the broadest and deepest possible way. You will be asked to identify a warehouse of goods ready to be put into use in the service of your eventual goals, and you may find a hidden stock of learning that is large and valuable.

How do you go about taking inventory of your skills and knowledge? As you reflect on different areas of skills and knowledge, the easiest place to begin in each area is with the most obvious, school learning. School learning is directed primarily toward the skills and subject matters (e.g., arithmetic, geography, physics, literature, anatomy, French, international business) learned in a formal educational setting. School knowledge began for most of us in kindergarten with reading and numbers and may reach such advanced levels as real estate law or materials science for those who have already completed or nearly completed a degree. Since at least one author claims that he learned everything he knows in kindergarten, when you take inventory, look at skills and other areas of learning besides college course titles and "book learning." You, too, undoubtedly learned more in school than course content.

Also consider what you have learned through experience as you do your inventory. Experiential learning takes place everywhere. It includes learning sports or dance, acquiring the skills of a master electrician as an on-the-job apprentice, learning a second language by living in a foreign country, studying poetry and writing your own, or learning how to lead a team as a result of your occupational tasks.

Experiential learning may be harder to identify than school learning because it is made up of subtly integrated physical and intellectual components—and all "physical" learning has an intellectual basis. Whereas school learning may focus on theoretical principles and abstract concepts, experiential learning can form a sturdy foundation for understanding and a way of applying those principles and concepts.

Higher-order learning meshes school with experiential learning; it requires the skills of gathering, organizing, and analyzing data in order to develop hypotheses. For example, higher-order learning takes some algorithm such as the Pythagorean Theorem and applies it to space travel. It combines all that you have learned in a class on the history of English literature and all that you have learned in your own experience as town alderman and produces an analysis of Shakespeare's King John that is rich and full of reality. Higher-order learning combines types of learning to develop and explore relationships among unlike ideas and apply learning to new situations.

Keep these types of learning in mind as you reflect on your skills and knowledge, and realize that you may have school, experiential, and/or higher-order learning in some areas.

Even though all knowledge is interrelated, the following inventory will ask you to divide your skills and knowledge into eight areas simply for "ease of handling." The eight areas are the following:

1. information gathering
2. observation
3. critical analysis, evaluation, and interpretation
4. quantitative reasoning and representation of numerical data
5. communication skills: listening, speaking, reading, writing
6. memory and visualization
7. time management
8. general knowledge

The first six areas include skills that are important to the act of learning, since they deal with methods of gathering, understanding, retaining, responding to, and communicating information. The seventh area, time management, is an important "management of learning" skill, since learning mainly occurs only as we take time to actively think about and process information. Time management essentially "clears the decks" for information gathering, observation and reflection, critical analysis, quantitative reasoning, communication, and/or visualization. The eighth area, general knowledge, differs from the other areas. As you identify general knowledge, you will not record your skills but *will* record the learning outcomes of those skills. Taken all together, the eight areas should provide you with an overall picture of yourself as a learner.

The Usefulness of an Inventory

As you begin the inventory, you may find it helpful to know that many students readily identify skills and knowledge acquired in a specific setting (job, school) and/or focused toward learning a specific topic or skill. Everyone also seems to remember those things that were especially hard to learn. What nearly everyone forgets are those skills used frequently in ordinary life and acquired almost by "osmosis." For example, you may write memos to colleagues at work so often that you forget that this represents a specific kind of communication skill. Or you may know that you are an exceptionally skilled driver, but neglect to include fast observation skills as part of your inventory. Remember to consider the "obvious," everyday skills and knowledge that you have acquired as well as the more specific learning related to work or school.

What about the things that you *don't* know? As you inventory your skills and knowledge, remember as well to identify those areas that you believe need further work and development. You may have no problem balancing your checkbook but cannot calculate compound interest easily. You may be able to write clear descriptive reports on clients' behavior but may never have had to analyze and evaluate the causes of that behavior. It's just as important to identify things that you don't know as well as things that you know, in order to get as complete a picture as possible of your current learning.

- Use the following questions for each area to spark your thoughts about your particular learning.
- Please do *not* simply "go down the list" in order to create your inventory; the questions are *not* designed for that kind of response.
- Instead, read the questions for each section first. Think about the questions in relation to your own learning. Then you can identify and list what you know and don't know in each of the eight areas on the appropriate inventory page.

Note: Your advisor may ask you to submit copies of your inventory pages as part of the assignment for this section. Discuss with advisor.

Assignment: Learning Portrait Essay

Write an essay that explains your learning. What is the current state of your learning? In what areas do you have the most skill and knowledge? The least? What aptitudes, interests, values, past learning experiences, and life or work needs account for your current skills and knowledge? As you can see, this essay asks you to synthesize or blend the information from the inventories into a coherent portrait of yourself as a learner that provides both description and interpretation of your learning.

You do not need to use every bit of information from the inventories in order to write this essay. Choose to present only the most important aspects of yourself as a learner, those aspects that most characterize you. The inventories should provide ample data for a three- to five-page essay. (Note that this is merely a general suggestion for essay length, to let you know that one page is not sufficient and twenty pages are not necessary. Any short essay length is fine.)

Assignment Objectives and Evaluation Criteria

- show ability to reflect carefully on your learning
- show ability to connect current learning to interests, capabilities, values, and past learning experiences
- show ability to articulate reflections in written form
- show ability to write coherently using standard essay form

Once you finish your learning portrait essay, you will have completed the required assignment and answered the first question of the self-assessment process. You should have quite a good understanding of the things that you know, don't know, and want to know at this point, an understanding that involves reasons why you have chosen to learn or not learn certain things, based on your interests, purposes, values, and past learning experiences.

Before you send your assignment to your advisor, though, you need to consider whether to do the assessment on prior college-level learning. Although you will specify and choose the appropriate credits to use toward your degree much more fully in Educational Planning 212, at this point you and your advisor may want to know in a general way what you have in your "bank" of credits that are potentially usable toward your degree, especially the credit-worthy learning that you may have gathered outside of formal college study (potential credit that is not readily apparent since it is not listed on a college transcript). This assessment is intended to identify the credit that you may have in that bank.

Review the next page and discuss your situation with your advisor to determine whether it makes sense for you to do the assessment. If you choose to do the assessment, then complete it as directed in the assessment packet entitled Prior College-Level Learning.

Appendix D

Program: Queen's Worker Education Program
Instructor: Paul Mischler (with Cara Murray)
Course: Labor Studies/News Article Writing
Topic: Solidarity Semester Project
Date: Spring 1997

Course Description

This Solidarity Semester Project will be an 8-credit course that will integrate labor studies, writing, and a practicum in labor/community. The focus of the project will be the campaign against sweatshops, which is being organized by UNITE! (Union of Needle trades, Industrial and Textile Employees). Its campaign includes organizing workers, building the justice centers, leading consumer boycotts, and educating the public about issues facing garment workers.

Through examining and participating in the campaigns of UNITE! students will look at long-term social historical, economic, and political problems facing the labor movement; and write both analytical and creative papers addressing the issues facing garment workers, as well as articles for union newspapers, church newsletters, and neighborhood newspapers. In the practicum segment of this course, students will meet with faculty and union activists to plan out a campaign of solidarity with garment workers within their community organization, church, union, or in another context chosen by students.

Students will be responsible for attending *all* classes, both Thursday evening and Saturday morning and engaging in a project around the issues facing garment workers today. Students are responsible for the reading, participating in class discussions, and writing projects in both the labor studies and writing modules. The final project will be a journal (see below).

Journal Project

The final project for the Solidarity Semester will be a journal. Entries in the journal will be made weekly. The journal may include writing projects for the Labor Studies and writing modules, letters to the editor, newspaper articles written by the students, and reflective writing on the projects engaged in by the students.

Labor Studies Module Meets Saturday
Mornings 9:30–12:15

In this section of the project we will look at the issues facing labor in both a local and world context through looking at a particular group of workers—New York City's garment workers. Since the late nineteenth century New York has been a center for the manufacture of clothing. Always a low-wage/low capital-investment sector of the economy, garment manufacturing has been composed of small shops with a largely immigrant work force. In the early twentieth century most of the workers were Jewish immigrants from Eastern Europe, with small groups of Italians and other nationalities. Many of the most unskilled workers were young women. The "sweatshop," born in this era as small enterprises, was at the mercy of the ups and downs of the market and used home work, long hours, and low pay to profit off the immigrant work force, who often had nowhere else to go.

These conditions led to the organization of unions in New Yorks garment industry. Two main unions organized garment workers: The International Ladies Garment Workers Union (ILGWU) for workers in women's garments, and the Amalgamated Clothing Workers of America (ACWA) for workers in men's garments. A smaller union, the Fur and Leather Workers Union, represented workers in the fur industry. In the 1970s, the ACWA merged with the International Textile Workers of America, and in 1995 the ILGWU and the Amalgamated Clothing and Textile Workers merged to form UNITE!—the Union of Needle trades, Industrial and Textile Employees.

The organization of the garment industry led to a certain stability in the garment industry. As the children of the early immigrants moved into jobs outside the industry after the Second World War, new immigrants replaced them during the 1950s and 1960s. By the end of the 1960s, changes in the world economy, national economic policy, and in New York's economy led many garment shops to leave New York in search of lower wages. First, industry moved to the southern United States—our own "third world"—where racism and concentrated political power kept wages low. Then garment factories moved to Latin America and Asia, which decimated the garment industry and this was one of the key ingredients in the loss of manufacturing jobs in New York over the past twenty years. The loss of manufacturing jobs in New York has had serious ripple effects throughout the city's economy. It changed both the tax base for public spending, led to loss of job opportunities for working-class New Yorkers, and increased the economic polarization that we all recognize as one of the features of the New World Order in the city.

Module III—Practicum-Solidarity Project

Each student will be required to engage in a solidarity project around the UNITE! campaign. Among possible projects can be building solidarity committees in unions, churches, and community organization; working with justice centers (if students have particular skills useful for the centers—we don't want students becoming a burden on the centers); organizing a letter-writing campaign in local newspapers about conditions in sweatshops; organizing a consumer boycott of targeted retailers such as Kmart, the Gap, etc.

Students will meet regularly with faculty members (to be chosen later) who can help guide the Solidarity Projects. This module on its own will not require extra readings—those will be in the other two modules. But it will require regular checkup and evaluation.

Students will be required to write a report of their Solidarity Project. This could be in the form of a journal, a report, and, possibly, a scrapbook of news reports on their activities. This report will be the final report for the entire project and encompass Labor Studies background, writing ability, and the work of the practicum.

Appendix E

Program: Queen's Worker Education Program
Instructor: Cara Murray (with Paul Mischler)
Course: Newspaper and Article Writing
Topic: Solidarity Projet
Date: Spring 1997

Course Description

The project of this class is to develop in students the tools that they need to think about and respond to the world around them through writing. The course is designed to produce in students a confidence in their ability to comment upon one of two subjects that affect labor today: the Work Experience Program or sweatshops. Through reading articles and reports that situate labor in the global economy, students will become experts on the current public discourse about labor issues. They will be asked to use this knowledge to respond to their own situations as workers, and will be encouraged to create spaces outside the classroom to get their ideas across. The course is divided into four sections based on types of writing found in newspapers: the feature story, the hard news article, the letter to the editor, and the review. In addition to writing one of each of these types of articles, students are expected to hand in their Solidarity Projects on the final day of class.

Part One—The Feature Story, The Summary

In weeks one through five, we will read two examples of the feature article: Charles Bowden's "While You Were Sleeping" and Ted C. Fishman's "The Joys of Global Investment—Shipping Home the Fruits of Misery." We will analyze the arguments presented by these two writers and come up with our own critiques of the writers' handling of the material. This section will culminate with students writing their own human interest story.

Part Two—Hard News, The Summary

None of the articles for this section of the class are set, for we will be following news stories as they unfold. Each student should choose one issue: sweatshops, Work Experience Program (WEP), and one newspaper. Let me know which paper and which issue you are choosing in advance. Also, we can expand the issue list if it would help you on your project. The student will be responsible for clipping stories from the paper and writing a one-paragraph summary of each story clipped.

Part Three—Letter to the Editor

This section will focus on getting students' educated opinion out there. Students should continue to collect newspaper articles on their chosen subject matter, but should now keep in mind a way to respond quickly to the public discourse about WEP or sweatshops. By now, students will have a file of clippings and should be armed to respond quickly to some story that catches their eye or the lack of story that catches their eye.

Part Four—The Review

In this section of the class, we will focus on various types of review writing. We will see the latest Mandela documentary, and review it. These reviews will be workshopped and used as examples for our final writing project, the book review. Students should have by week eleven discovered which book they would like to review.

Appendix F

Program: Swingshift College
Instructor: Doug Swartz
Topic: Writing About Working-Class Literature
Date: January 27, 1998

Topics for a Narrative or Descriptive Essay

On January 26, the class brainstormed ideas for writing that imitates Ben Hamper's *Rivethead* in some way. Many of the things Hamper wrote about are things the class said they could identify with. Many people took vehement exception to Hamper's depiction of factory life. The general assignment is to write a narrative or descriptive essay prompted by your reading of Hamper. Here are some specific suggestions:

1. Hamper writes frequently about the ongoing and universal struggle of the factory worker to beat the clock. Describe your experience of time on the job and your and your coworkers' attempts to make time pass.

2. After describing his attendance at a "State of the Factory" meeting, Hamper writes, "Why would any of us give a shit about the specifics of the grand master plan? We knew what holes our screws went in. That was truth enough for us" (47). Does that describe your attitude toward your work and its place in "something larger"?

3. Hamper often alludes to his and his coworkers' feeling of the inevitability of their becoming autoworkers, calling (not of course without irony) it a "birthright" and a "heritage." Write a "hiring-in" story of your own. How did you come to do the work that you do? Was it a choice deliberately made, or as Hamper suggests his was, made by default? You might also write about the initiation process that goes on for new hires, either as you experienced it or as you have observed it.

4. Write an essay on the "You're not paid to think" syndrome. Hamper often writes about "idiot labor" and suggests that factory work deadens thought. Do you agree? You might write about the thinking that

goes with your job, along with the struggles you may have to receive acknowledgement for that thought.

5. Hamper makes a satirical target of hapless Howie Maken, the Quality Cat. Describe similar programs you have encountered on the job and analyze their significance or effectiveness.

6. Hamper describes "the many bizarre individuals" he met during his time at GM. Do a personality profile of some admirable or eccentric person where you work.

7. Describe some of the pranks and practical jokes that go on in your workplace and discuss how they function as coping strategies.

8. Discuss relationships between sexes and among races and cultures in your work.

Appendix G

Program: Youngstown State University
Instructors: Kelly Belanger and Jan Kotwis (Institute for Career
              Development coordinator)
Course: First-Year and Intermediate Composition (Mixed Place-
              ment Levels)
Topic: Reading, Writing, and Teaching Life Experience
Date: Winter 1998

Course Description

Since birth, we have all been gathering knowledge and skills related to a variety of subjects just by living our lives. Experiential learning, as it is sometimes called, occurs in many forms. The following is a list of just a few activities that could be a source of learning: working with groups as a member of a union, running a household or business, caring for children or aging parents, and traveling overseas. Through a series of reading and writing assignments, in this course, you will explore what you have learned through life experience; then we will select an area of expertise that you might like to teach to other adults; you will write and implement a lesson plan(s) for a workshop or series of workshops; finally, you will compose a research essay that develops an argument on a topic of your choosing that incorporates both academic and experiential knowledge.

Part of this course will take place via the Internet. If you don't already have an e-mail account, you will get one and learn how to access our course Web page on the Internet. On occasion, we will not meet face to face as a class; instead, you will participate in an on-line discussion through a course list-serve. If you aren't familiar with e-mail and the Internet, don't worry! It's a fun and convenient way to discuss ideas, gather information, or just keep in touch with me and your classmates. I'll make sure everyone is ready before we hold our first on-line class session.

Assignments

- a portfolio of informal writings in which you explore your life experience and respond to reading assignments
- a three- to five-page Learning Portrait Essay that describes in detail your personal learning processes
- an annotated bibliography on the topic you want to teach
- a lesson plan with rationale
- a researched essay on some issue related to your topic (required for intermediate composition students only)

Bibliography

Adams, F., with M. Horton. 1975. *Unearthing Seeds of Fire: The Idea of Highlander.* Winston-Salem, N.C.: John F. Blair.

Allen, R. 1962. "Resident Study Program for Union Staff." In *Orientation in Labor Education: A Symposium on Liberal Education for Labor in the University,* ed. F. H. Goldman, 61–73. Chicago: Center for the Study of Liberal Education for Adults.

Altenbaugh, R. J. 1990. *Education for Struggle: The American Labor Colleges of the 1920s and 1930s.* Philadelphia: Temple University Press.

American Federation of Labor. 1954. *Labor and Education in 1953: Reports of the Executive Council and the Annual Convention of the American Federation of Labor on Education in 1953.* Washington, D.C.

Archer, J. W., and W. A. Ferrell, eds. 1965. *Research and the Development of English Programs in the Junior College.* Champaign, Ill.: National Council of Teachers of English.

Aronowitz, S., and H. A. Giroux. 1985. *Education Under Siege: The Conservative, Liberal, and Radical Debate over Schooling.* South Hadley, Mass.: Bergin & Garvery.

Autry, J. 1994. *Life and Work: A Manager's Search for Meaning.* New York: Avon.

Bacon, E. 1962. "Fourth Year Institute: The World of Ideas." In *Orientation in Labor Education: A Symposium on Liberal Education for Labor in the University,* ed. F. H. Goldman, 43–49. Chicago: Center for the Study of Liberal Education for Adults.

Bartholomae, D. 1988. "Inventing the University." In *Perspectives on Literacy,* ed. E. R. Kintgen, B. Kroll, and M. Rose, 273–85. Carbondale and Edwardsville, Ill.: Southern Illinois University Press.

Bartholomae, D., and A. Petrosky. 1986. *Facts, Artifacts, and Counterfacts.* Upper Montclair, N.J.: Boynton.

———, eds. 1996. *Ways of Reading: An Anthology for Writers.* Boston: Bedford/ St. Martins.

Bateson, M. C. 1996. *Composing a Life.* New York: Penguin Books.

Bauder, P. D. 1952. "Freshman English Experiment: General Education in a Traditional Curriculum." *Junior College Journal* 22 (6): 337–39.

Belanger, K., L. Strom, and J. Russo. 1997. "Critical Literacy and the Organizing Model of Unionism: Reading and Writing History At a Steelworkers' Union Hall." *Radical Teacher* 51: 16–21.

Bell, T. 1976. *Out of This Furnace.* Pittsburgh: University of Pittsburgh Press.

Bergmann, F. 1992. "The Future of Work." In *Working in America: A Humanities Reader.* eds. R. Sessions and J. Wortman, 11–27. South Bend, Ind.: University of Notre Dame Press.

Berlin, J. 1987. *Rhetoric and Reality: Writing Instruction in American Colleges, 1900–1985.* Carbondale, Ill.: Southern Illinois University Press.

———. 1988. "Rhetoric and Ideology in the Writing Class." *College English* 50 (5): 477–94.

———. 1990. "Writing Instruction in School and College English, 1890–1985." In *A Short History of Writing Instruction: From Ancient Greece to Twentieth-Century America,* ed. J. Murphy, 183–220. Davis, Calif.: Hermagoras Press.

———. 1996. *Rhetorics, Poetics, and Cultures: Refiguring College English Studies.* Urbana, Ill.: National Council of Teachers of English.

Bizzell, P. 1986. "What Happens When Basic Writers Come to College?" *College Composition and Communication* 37 (3): 294–301.

———. 1992. *Academic Discourse and Critical Consciousness.* Pittsburgh: University of Pittsburgh Press.

Bloom, L. Z., D. A. Daiker, and E. M. White, eds. 1996. *Composition in the Twenty-First Century: Crisis and Change.* Carbondale, Ill.: Southern Illinois University Press.

Bode, C. 1956. *The American Lyceum: Town Meeting of the Mind.* New York: Oxford University Press.

Boydston, J., ed. 1976. *The Middle Works of John Dewey, 1899–1924.* Vol. 9. Carbondale and Edwardsville, Ill.: Southern Illinois University Press.

Boyer, E. L. 1983. *High School: A Report on Secondary Education.* New York: Harper & Row.

Brecher, J. 1988. *History from Below: How to Uncover and Tell the Story of Your Community, Association, or Union.* New Haven, Conn.: Advocate.

Brody, D. 1987. "The Origins of Modern Steel Unionism." In *Forging a Union of Steel: Philip Murray, SWOC, and the United Steelworkers,* ed. P. F. Clark, P. Gottlieb, and D. Kennedy, 13–29. Ithaca, N.Y.: ILR Press.

Brooke, R. 1988. "Modeling a Writer's Identity: Reading and Imitation in the Writing Classroom." *College Composition and Communication* 39 (1): 23–41.

Brown, C. 1974. "Literacy in 30 Hours: Paulo Freire's Process in Northeast Brazil." *Social Policy* 5 (2): 25–32.

Brown, E. L. 1955. "Teaching Sophomore Literature: Conference Method." *College English* 16 (5): 296–302.

Buffington, N., and C. Moneyhun. 1997. "A Conversation with Gerald Graff and Ira Shor." *Journal of Advanced Composition* 17 (1): 1–21.

Brubaker, D. 1995. "From the President's Desk." *The Warren Steelworker* 2 (1): 2.

Byington, M. 1969. *Homestead: The Households of a Mill Town.* New York: Arno.

Campbell, R. 1962. "Education and Leadership Development—Challenges to Labor Education." In *Challenges to Labor Education in the 60's,* 56–68. Washington, D.C.: National Institute of Labor Education.

Carlson, G. R. 1949. "The Contributions of English to Home and Family Living." *Junior College Journal* 20 (4): 209–17.

Charters, A., and S. Charters. 1997. *Literature and Its Writers: An Introduction to Fiction, Poetry, and Drama.* Boston: Bedford Books.

Chase, G. 1988. "Accommodation, Resistance and the Politics of Student Writing." *College Composition and Communication* 39 (1): 13–22.

Chordas, N. 1992. "Classroom, Pedagogies, and the Rhetoric of Equality." *College Composition and Communication* 43 (2): 214–24.

Clifford, J., and J. Schilb, eds. 1994. *Writing Theory and Critical Theory.* New York: The Modern Language Association of America.

Coles, N., and S. V. Wall. 1987. "Conflict and Power in the Reader-Responses of Adult Basic Writers." *College English* 49 (3): 298–314.

Coles, R. 1976. "Work and Self-Respect." *Daedalus* 105: 29–38.

Cook, C. K. 1985. *How to Improve Your Own Writing.* New York: Houghton Mifflin.

Creighton, Aileen. 1965. "English Courses for Adults and Community Services." In *Research and the Development of English Programs in the Junior College,* ed. J. W. Archer and W. A. Ferrell, 83–90. Champaign, Ill.: National Council of Teachers of English.

Cross, N. 1961. "Current Status of the Two-Year College." *College Composition and Communication* 22 (3): 131–33.

Curoe, P. R. V. 1926. *Educational Attitudes and Policies of Organized Labor in the United States.* New York: Teachers College, Columbia University.

Dewey, J. 1916. "Democracy and Education" In *The Middle Works of John Dewey, 1899–1924,* ed. J. Boydston. Carbondale and Edwardsville, Ill.: Southern Illinois Press. Reprinted from the MacMillan Company.

Dougherty, K. J. 1994. *The Contradictory College: The Conflicting Origins, Impacts, and Futures of the Community College.* New York: State University of New York Press.

Elias, J. L. 1994. *Paulo Freire: Pedagogue of Liberation.* Malabar, Fl.: Krieger.

Elbow, P. 1986. *Embracing Contraries: Explorations in Learning and Teaching.* New York: Oxford University Press.

———. 1990. "Forward: About Personal Expressive Academic Writing." *PRE/TEXT* 11 (1–2): 7–20.

———. 1991. "Some Thoughts on *Expressive Discourse:* A Review Essay." Review of *Expressive Discourse,* by J. Harris. *Journal of Advanced Composition* 11 (1): 83–93.

Ellsworth, E. 1989. "Why Doesn't This Feel Empowering? Working Through the Repressive Myths of Critical Pedagogy." *Harvard Educational Review* 59 (3): 297–324.

Erickson, F. 1988. "Literacy, Reasoning, and Civility." In *Perspectives on Literacy*, ed. E. R. Kintgen, B. Kroll, and M. Rose, 207–26. Carbondale and Edwardsville, Ill.: Southern Illinois University Press.

Eschholz, P., and A. Rosa, eds. 1995. *Outlooks and Insights: A Reader for College Writers*. 4th ed. New York: St. Martins Press.

Faculty Guide for LSHU 310: Interpreting Experience. 1997. Redlands, Ca.: University of Redlands/Whitehead College, Dept. of Liberal Studies.

Farmer, J. A., Jr. 1972. "Adult Education for Transiting." In *Paulo Freire: A Revolutionary Dilemma for the Adult Educator*, ed. S. M. Grabowsri, 1–12. Syracuse, N.Y.: ERIC Clearinghouse on Adult Education.

Feiler, B. 1991. *Learning to Bow*. New York: Ticknor & Fields.

Fiore, K., and N. Elsasser. 1988. "'Strangers No More': A Liberatory Literacy Curriculum." In *Perspectives on Literacy*, ed. E. R. Kintgen, B. Kroll, and M. Rose, 286–99. Carbondale and Edwardsville, Ill.: Southern Illinois University Press.

Fisher, B. E. 1951. "Communications, a Year's Work." *Junior College Journal* 22 (2): 86–89.

———. 1951. "Communications Courses for Junior Colleges." *Junior College Journal* 21 (5): 289–91.

Fishman, S. M., and L. P. McCarthy. 1992. "Is Expressivism Dead? Reconsidering Its Romantic Roots and Its Relation to Social Contructionism." *College English* 54 (6): 647–61.

Fitts, K., and A. W. France, eds. 1995. *Left Margins: Cultural Studies and Composition Pedagogy*. New York: State University of New York Press.

Flower, L. 1981. *Problem-Solving Strategies for Writing*. New York: Harcourt Brace Jovanovich.

———. 1994. *The Construction of Negotiated Meaning: A Social Cognitive Theory of Writing*. Carbondale and Edwardsville, Ill.: Southern Illinios University Press.

Flower, L., J. Ackerman, M. J. Kantz, K. McCormick, W. C. Peck, and V. Stein. 1990. *Reading-to-Write: Exploring a Cognitive and Social Process*. New York: Oxford University Press.

Fox, T. J. 1990. *The Social Uses of Writing: Politics and Pedagogy*. Norwood, N.J.: Ablex.

Fraiberg, A. 1997. *Faculty Resource Guide for English 301*. Redlands, Calif.: University of Redlands/Alfred North Whitehead College.

Freebody, P., and A. R. Welch, eds. 1993. *Knowledge, Culture and Power: International Perspectives on Literacy as Policy and Practice*. Pittsburgh: University of Pittsburgh Press.

Freire, P. 1970a. "The Adult Literacy Process as Cultural Action for Freedom." Trans. L. Stover. *Harvard Educational Review* 40 (2): 205–25.

———. 1970b. *Pedagogy of the Oppressed*. Trans. M. B. Ramos. New York: Continuum.

————. 1973. *Education for Critical Consciousness.* New York: Seabury Press.

————. 1978. *Pedagogy in Process: The Letters to Guinea-Bissau.* Trans. C. St. John Hunter. New York: Seabury Press.

————. 1985. *The Politics of Education: Culture, Power, and Liberation.* Trans. D. Macedo. New York: Bergin & Garvey.

————. 1988. "The Adult Literacy Process as Cultural Action for Freedom and Education and Conscientizacao." In *Perspectives on Literacy,* ed. E. R. Kintgen, B. Kroll, and M. Rose, 398–409. Carbondale and Edwardsville, Ill.: Southern Illinois University Press.

————. 1989. *Learning to Question: A Pedagogy of Liberation.* New York: Continuum.

————. 1996. *Letters to Cristina: Reflections on My Life and Work.* Trans. D. Macedo with Q. Macedo and A. Oliveira. New York: Routledge.

Freire, P., and D. Macedo. 1987. *Literacy: Reading the Word and the World.* South Hadley, Mass: Bergin & Garvey.

Fueyo, J. M. 1988. "Technical Literacy Versus Critical Literacy in Adult Basic Education." *Journal of Education* 170 (1): 107–18.

Garrison, R. H. 1971. "Teaching Liberal Arts in the Junior College." In *Perspectives on the Community-Junior College,* ed. W. K. Ogilvie and M. R. Raines, 232–33. New York: Merideth Corporation.

Gere, A. R. 1997. *Initimate Practices: Literacy and Cultural Work in U.S. Women's Clubs, 1880–1920.* Urbana, Ill.: University of Illinois Press.

Girdler, T. 1943. *Bootstraps.* New York: Scribners.

Goldman, F. H., ed. 1962. *Reorientation in Labor Education: A Symposium on Liberal Education for Labor in the University.* Chicago: Center for the Study of Liberal Education for Adults.

Goldwin, R. A., ed. 1965. *Higher Education and Modern Democracy: The Crisis of the Few and the Many.* Chicago: Rand McNally & Company.

Goleman, J. 1987. "Getting There: A Freshman Course in Social Dialectics." *Journal of Education* 169 (3): 48–57.

Gould, A. L. 1962. "Liberal Arts for Labor." In *Orientation in Labor Education: A Symposium on Liberal Education for Labor in the University,* ed. F. H. Goldman. 25–41. Chicago: Center for the Study of Liberal Education for Adults.

Grabowski, M. 1972. *Paulo Freire: A Revolutionary Dilemma for the Adult Educator.* Syracuse, N.Y.: ERIC Clearinghouse on Adult Education.

Graff, G. 1992. *Beyond the Culture Wars: How Teaching the Conflicts Can Revitalize American Education.* New York: Norton.

Graff, H. J. 1981. *Literacy in History: An Interdisciplinary Research Bibliography.* New York: Garland.

Green, B., ed. 1993. *The Insistence of the Letter: Literacy Studies and Curriculum Theorizing.* Pittsburgh: University of Pittsburgh Press.

Greene, M. 1986. "In Search of a Critical Pedagogy." *Harvard Educational Review* 56 (4): 427–41.

Gregory, G. W. 1958. "Approach to Functional English in a Four-Year Junior College." *Junior College Journal* 29 (5): 203–205.

Guthrie, R., P. C. Olson, and D. M. Schaeffer. 1997. "The Professor as Tele-worker." In *The Virtual Workplace,* ed. M. Igbaria and M. Tan. Harrisburg, Pa.: Idea Publishing Group.

Hairston, M. 1992. "Diversity, Ideology, and Teaching Writing." *College Composition and Communication* 43 (2): 179–93.

Hall, G. 1987. *Working Class USA: The Power and the Movement.* New York: International.

Hall, S., and M. Jacques, eds. 1990. *New Times: The Changing Face of Politics in the 1990s.* London: Verso.

Hamper, B. 1991. *Rivethead: Tales from the Assembly Line.* New York: Warner Books.

Hansome, M. 1968. *World Workers' Educational Movements: Their Social Significance.* New York: AMS Press.

Harris, J. 1990. *Expressive Discourse.* Dallas: Southern Methodist University Press.

Harris, M. 1995. "Talking in the Middle: Why Writers Need Writing Tutors." *College English* 57 (1): 27–43.

Heath, S. B. 1996. "Work, Class, and Categories: Dilemmas of Identity." *Composition in the Twenty-First Century: Crisis and Change,* ed. L. Z. Bloom, D. A. Daiker, and E. M. White, 226–42. Carbondale and Edwardsville, Ill.: Southern Illinois University Press.

Heilker, P., and P. Vandenberg. 1996. *Keywords in Composition Studies.* Portsmouth, N.H.: Boynton/Cook.

Hollinger, D., and C. Capper, eds. 1992. *The American Intellectual Tradition.* 2d ed. 2 vols. New York and Oxford: Oxford University Press.

Hollis, K. 1988. "Building a Context for Critical Literacy: Student Writers as Critical Theorists." *The Writing Instructor* 7 (3–4): 122–30.

———. 1994. "Autobiographical Writing at the Bryn Mawr School for Women Workers." *College Composition and Communication* 45 (1): 31–60.

Holzman, M. 1988. "A Post-Freirean Model for Adult Literacy Education." *College English* 50 (2): 177–89.

Hourigan, M. 1994. *Literacy as Social Exchange: Intersections of Class, Gender, and Culture.* New York: State University of New York Press.

Howlett, C. F. 1993. *Brockwood Labor College and the Struggle for Peace and Social Justice in America.* Lewiston, N.Y.: The Edwin Mellen Press.

Hull, G., ed. 1997. *Changing Work, Changing Workers: Critical Pespectives on Language, Literacy, and Skills.* New York: State University of New York Press.

Hull, G., M. Castellano, K. L. Fraser, and M. Rose. 1991. "Remediation as Social Construct: Perspectives from an Analysis of Classroom Discourse." *College Composition and Communication* 42 (3): 299–327.

Hull, G., and M. Rose. 1989. "Rethinking Remediation: Toward a Social-Cognitive Understanding of Problematic Reading and Writing." *Written Communication* 6 (2): 139–55.

————. 1990. "'This Wooden Shack Place': The Logic of an Unconventional Reading." *College Composition and Communication* 41 (2): 287–98.

Hurlbert, M. C., and M. Blitz. 1991. *Composition and Resistance.* Portsmouth, N.H.: Boynton/Cook.

Jones, A. P. 1954. "Freshman Studies: An Experimental Course at Lawrence College." *The Educational Record* 35 (2): 208–20.

Kates, S. L. 1995. "Critical Pedagogy and Educational History: Rhetorical Instruction at Three Non-Traditional Colleges, 1884–1937." Dissertation, the Ohio State University.

Kelley, P., and D. Wallace. 1986. "A Technology of the Intellect? Reflections on Literacy and Ideology." *The Writing Instructor* 5 (3): 139–46.

Kerrison, I. L. H. 1951. *Workers' Education at the University Level.* New Brunswick, N.J.: Rutgers University Press.

————. 1962. "The Institute Labor Program." In *Orientation in Labor Education: A Symposium on Liberal Education for Labor in the University,* ed. F. H. Goldman, 51–59. Chicago: Center for the Study of Liberal Education for Adults.

Kerrison, I. L. H., and H. A. Levine. 1960. *Labor Leadership Education.* New Brunswick, N.J.: Rutgers University Press.

Kintgen, E. R., B. Kroll, and M. Rose. 1988. *Perspectives on Literacy.* Carbondale, Ill.: Southern Illinois University Press.

Kirsch, G., and P. A. Sullivan. 1992. *Methods and Methodology in Composition Research.* Carbondale and Edwardsville, Ill.: Southern Illinois University Press.

Kiskis, M. J. 1994. "Adult Learners, Autobiography, and Educational Planning: Reflections on Pedagogy, Andragogy, and Power." In *Pedagogy in the Age of Politics: Writing and Reading (in) the Academy,* ed. P. A. Sullivan and D. J. Qualley, 56–72. Urbana, Ill.: National Council of Teachers of English.

Kitzhaber, A. 1965. "English Instruction in Two-Year Colleges: Problems and Possibilities." In *Research and the Development of English Programs in the Junior College,* ed. J. W. Archer and W. A. Ferrell, 2. Champaign, Ill.: National Council of Teachers of English.

Knoblauch, C. H. 1988. "Rhetorical Constructions: Dialogue and Commitment." *College English* 50 (2): 125–40.

Knoblauch, C. H., and L. Brannon. 1993. *Critical Teaching and the Idea of Literacy.* Portsmouth, N.H.: Boynton/Cook.

Knowles, M. S., ed. 1969. *Higher Adult Education in the United States.* Washington, D.C.: American Council on Education.

Kornbluh, H., 1962. "Survey of Non-University Connected Liberal Education for Trade Unionists." In *Orientation in Labor Education: A Symposium on Liberal Education for Labor in the University,* ed. F. H. Goldman, 89–99. Chicago: Center for the Study of Liberal Education for Adults.

Kornbluh, J. L. 1987. *A New Deal for Workers' Education: The Worker' Service Program, 1933–1942.* Urbana, Ill.: University of Illinois Press.

Kornbluh, J. L., and M. Frederickson, eds. 1984. *Sisterhood and Solidarity: Workers' Education for Women, 1914–1984.* Philadelphia: Temple University Press.

Kozol, J. 1991. *Savage Inequalities: Children in Americas Schools.* New York: Crown.

Kubler-Ross, E. 1969. *On Death and Dying.* New York: Macmillan.

Langford, H. D. 1936. *Education and the Social Conflict.* New York: MacMillan Company.

Lankshear, C., and P. L. McLaren, eds. 1993. *Critical Literacy: Politics, Praxis, and the Postmodern.* Albany, N.Y.: State University of New York Press.

Lazere, D. 1992a. "Back to Basics: A Force for Oppression or Liberation?" *College English* 54 (1): 7–21.

———. 1992b. "Teaching the Political Conflicts: A Rhetorical Schema." *College Composition and Communication* 43 (2): 194–213.

———. 1995. "Teaching the Conflicts About Wealth and Poverty." In *Left Margins: Cultural Studies and Composition Pedagogy,* ed. K. Fitts and A. W. France, 189–205. New York: State University of New York Press.

Lee, J. 1994. *A World of Ideas: Essential Readings for College Writers.* Boston: Bedford/St. Martins.

LePage, W. L. 1968. *To Add to the Sum Total of Human Knowledge: The Story of Research at the Franklin Institute, 1824–1968.* New York: The Newcomen Society in North America.

Levine, A., and J. S. Cureton. 1998. "Collegiate Life: An Obituary." *Change: The Magazine of Higher Education* 30 (3): 12–17.

Liveright, A. A. 1962. "A Summary of Problems and Directions." In *Orientation in Labor Education: A Symposium on Liberal Education for Labor in the University,* ed. F. H. Goldman, 111–17. Chicago: Center for the Study of Liberal Education for Adults.

London, J. 1962. "Labor Education and the Universities." In *Orientation in Labor Education: A Symposium on Liberal Education for Labor in the University,* ed. F. H. Goldman, 11–23. Chicago: Center for the Study of Liberal Education for Adults.

London, J., and J. B. Ewing. 1982. "Adult Education and the Phenomena of Social Change." *Adult Education* 32 (4): 229–47.

Lovett, T., ed. 1988. *Radical Approaches to Adult Education: A Reader.* London and New York: Routledge.

Lucia, C. 1996. "First a Troublemaker, then a Troubleshooter." In *Rocking the Boat: Union Women's Voices, 1915–1975,* ed. B. O'Farrell and J. L. Kornbluh, 34–57. New Brunswick, N.J.: Rutgers University Press.

Lunsford, A., H. Moglen, and J. Slevin. 1990. *The Right to Literacy.* New York: The Modern Language Association of America.

Mackie, R. 1981. *Literacy and Revolution: The Pedagogy of Paulo Freire.* New York: Continuum.

Mantsios, G. 1995. "Living and Learning: Some Reflections on Emergence from and Service to the Working Class." In *Liberating Memory: Our Work and Our*

Working-Class Consciousness, ed. J. Zandy, 230–48. New Brunswick, N.J.: Rugters University Press.

Mazurek, R. A. "Freirean Pedagogy, Cultural Studies, and the Initiation of Students to Academic Discourse." In *Left Margins: Cultural Studies and Composition Pedagogy,* ed. K. Fitts and A. W. France, 173–87. New York: State University of New York Press.

McChesney, M. L. 1956. "Stimulating Enthusiasm for Creative Writing." *Junior College Journal* 27 (1): 48–49.

McClusky, H. Y. 1962. "What Lessons Has Adult Education Taught Us About Educational Methodology?" *Challenges to Labor Education in the 60's.* Washington, D.C.: National Institute of Labor Education. 70–78.

McCollum, J. 1962. "Union Leadership Program." In *Orientation in Labor Education: A Symposium on Liberal Education for Labor in the University,* ed. F. H. Goldman, 75–87. Chicago: Center for the Study of Liberal Education for Adults.

McLaren, P., and P. Leonard, eds. 1993. *Paulo Freire: A Critical Encounter.* New York: Routledge.

McLeod, A. 1986. "Critical Literacy: Taking Control of Our Own Lives." *Language Arts* 63 (1): 37–50.

Metzger, D. 1992. *Writing for Your Life: A Guide and Companion to the Inner Worlds.* San Francisco: Harper.

Mezirow, J. 1978. "Perspective Transformation." *Adult Education* 28 (2): 100–110.

Mezirow, J., et al. 1990. *Fostering Critical Reflection in Adulthood: A Guide to Transformative and Emancipatory Learning.* San Francisco: Jossey-Bass.

Mire, J. 1956. *Labor Education: A Study Report on Needs, Programs, and Approaches.* Madison, Wis.: Inter-University Labor Education Committee.

Moody, J. C., and A. Kesler-Harris. 1989. *Perspectives on American Labor History: The Problems of Synthesis.* DeKalb, Ill.: Northern Illinois University Press.

Moriarity, P., and N. Wallerstein. 1979. "Student/Teacher/Learner: A Freirean Approach to ABE/ESL." *Adult Literacy and Basic Education* 3 (2): 193–200.

National Institute of Labor Education. 1962. *Challenges to Labor Education in the 60's.* Washington, D.C.

North, S. M. 1987. *The Making of Knowledge in Composition: Portrait of an Emerging Field.* Portsmouth, N.H.: Boynton/Cook-Heinemann.

Oaks, S. 1991. *Self-Assessment: Writing.* Saratoga Springs, N.Y.: Center for Distance Learning, SUNY Empire State College.

Oaks, S., and T. Dehner. 1996. *Educational Planning Guide.* Saratoga Springs, N.Y.: Center for Distance Learning, SUNY Empire State College.

O'Farrell, B., and J. L. Kornbluh, eds. 1996. *Rocking the Boat: Union Women's Voices, 1915–1975.* New Brunswick, N.J.: Rutgers University Press.

Olson, G. A., and I. Gale. 1991. *(Inter)views: Cross Disciplinary Perspectives on Rhetoric and Literacy.* Carbondale and Edwardsville, Ill.: Southern Illinois University Press.

Peterson, E. 1996. "You Can't Giddyup by Saying Whoa." In *Rocking the Boat: Union Women's Voices, 1915–1975*, ed. B. O'Farrell and J. L. Kornbluh, 58–83. New Brunswick, N.J.: Rutgers University Press.

Pincus, F. L. 1986. "Vocational Education: Crisis in Credibility." In *Growth of an American Invention: A Documentary History of the Junior and Community College Movement*, ed. T. Diener, 217–27. New York: Greenwood Press.

Portfolio Guide for Management 310: Liberal Studies-Humanities 310 and Liberal Studies-Interdisciplinary Studies 310. 1997. Redlands, Calif.: University of Redlands/Alfred North Whitehead College.

Raines, H. H. 1993. "Reseeing the Past, Recounting the Present, Envisioning the Future: The Teaching of English in the Two-Year College." *Teaching English in the Two-Year College* 20 (2): 100–108.

Rechtschaffen, S. 1996. *Time Shifting: Creating More Time to Enjoy Your Life*. New York: Doubleday.

Resnick, D. P., and L. B. Resnick. 1977. "The Nature of Literacy: An Historical Exploration." *Harvard Educational Review* 47 (3): 370–85.

Robertson, C. A. 1997. *A Brief History of Whitehead*. Redlands, Calif.: University of Redlands.

Robins, A. 1996. *Analytical Writer: A College Rhetoric*. San Diego: Collegiate Press.

Rogin, L. 1962. "The Unions and Liberal Education for Labor." In *Orientation in Labor Education: A Symposium on Liberal Education for Labor in the University*, ed. F. H. Goldman, 5–10. Chicago: Center for the Study of Liberal Education for Adults.

Rose, M. 1987. "Remedial Writing Courses: A Critique and a Proposal." In *A Sourcebook for Basic Writing Teachers*, ed. T. Enos. New York: Random House.

———. 1989. *Lives on the Boundary: A Moving Account of the Struggles and Achievements of America's Educational Underclass*. New York: Penguin Books.

Ruggiero, V. R. 1995. *Beyond Feelings: A Guide to Critical Thinking*. Mountain View, Calif.: Mayfield.

Sessions, R., and J. Wortman, eds. 1992. *Working in America: A Humanities Reader*. South Bend, Ind.: University of Notre Dame Press.

Shaughnessy, M. P. 1979. *Errors & Expectations: A Guide for the Teacher of Basic Writing*. New York: Oxford University Press.

Shor, I. 1980. *Critical Teaching and Everday Life*. Boston: South End Press.

———. 1986. *Culture Wars: School and Society in the Conservative Restoration, 1969–1984*. Boston: Routledge & Kegan Paul.

———. 1987a. *Critical Teaching and Everyday Life*. Chicago: The University of Chicago Press.

———. 1987b. *Freire for the Classroom: A Sourcebook for Liberatory Teaching*. Portsmouth, N.H.: Boynton/Cook.

———. 1992. *Empowering Education: Critical Teaching for Social Change*. Chicago: University of Chicago Press.

———. 1993. "Education Is Politics: Paulo Freire's Critical Pedagogy." In *Paulo Freire: A Critical Encounter,* ed. P. McLaren and P. Leonard. London and New York: Routledge.

———. 1996. *When Students Have Power.* Chicago: University of Chicago Press.

Shor, I., and P. Freire. 1987. *A Pedagogy for Liberation: Dialogues on Transforming Education.* South Hadley, Mass.: Bergin & Garvey.

Shostak, M. 1981. *The Life and Works of a !Kung Woman.* Cambridge, Mass.: Harvard University Press.

Sinclair, B. 1974. *Philadelphia's Philosopher Mechanics: A History of the Franklin Institute: 1824–1865.* Baltimore: The Johns Hopkins University Press.

Sizer, T. 1985. *Horace's Compromise: The Dilemma of the American High School.* Boston: Houghton Mifflin.

Sommer, R. F. 1989. *Teaching Writing to Adults: Strategies and Concepts for Improving Learner Performance.* San Francisco: Jossey-Bass.

Street, B. V. 1995. *Social Literacies: Critical Approaches to Literacy in Development, Ethnography and Education.* London and New York: Longman.

Strom, L., and K. Belanger. 1996. "Teaching on 'Turns': Taking Composition Courses to a Union Hall." *The Writing Instructor* 15 (2): 71–82.

Sullivan, P. A., and D. J. Qualley, eds. 1994. *Pedagogy in the Age of Politics: Writing and Reading (in) the Academy.* Urbana, Ill.: National Council of Teachers.

SUNY Empire State College Bulletin: 1995–1997. 1995. Saratoga Springs, N.Y.: Office of Admissions, SUNY Empire State College.

Swerdlow, M. 1962. "Liberal Education in Canadian Labor Education." In *Orientation in Labor Education: A Symposium on Liberal Education for Labor in the University,* ed. F. H. Goldman, 101–9. Chicago: Center for the Study of Liberal Education for Adults.

Terkel, S. 1974. *Working: People Talk About What They Do All Day and How They Feel About What They Do.* New York: Pantheon Books.

Trimbur, J. 1994. "The Politics of Radical Pedagogy: A Plea for 'A Dose of Vulgar Marxism.'" Review of *Border Crossing: Cultural Workers and the Politics of Education,* by H. A. Giroux, *Beyond the Culture Wars: How Teaching the Conflicts Can Revitalize American Education,* by G. Graff, *Composition and Resistance,* by C. M. Hurlbert, *Empowering Education,* by I. Shor, and *Education Limited: Schooling and Training and the New Right Since 1979,* Education Group II, Cultural Studies, University of Birmingham. *College English* 56 (2): 194–204.

Tuman, M. C. 1988. "Class, Codes, and Composition: Basil Bernstein and the Critique of Pedagogy." *College Composition and Communication* 39 (1): 42–51.

Walker, A. 1983. *In Search of Our Mother's Gardens: A Womanist Prose.* San Diego: Harcourt Brace Jovanovich.

Walsh, C., ed. 1991. *Literacy as Praxis: Culture, Language, and Pedagogy.* Norwood, N.J.: Ablex.

Walvoord, B. E., L. P. McCarthy, V. J. Anderson, J. R. Breihan, S. M. Robinson, and A. K. Sherman. 1990. *Thinking and Writing in College: A Naturalistic Study of Students in Four Disciplines*. Urbana, Ill.: National Council of Teachers of English.

Weaver, F. S. 1991. *Liberal Education: Critical Essays on Professions, Pedagogy, and Structure*. New York: Teachers College Press.

Werthheimer, B. M. 1981. *Labor Education for Women Workers*. Philadelphia: Temple University Press.

Whitehead, A. N. 1968. *The Aims of Education and Other Essays*. New York: The Free Press.

Whiteman, M. F., ed. 1982. *Variation in Writing: Functional and Linguistic Cultural Differences. Vol. 1. Writing: The Nature, Development, and Teaching of Written Communication Series*. Hillsdale, N.J.: Erlbaum.

Wiener, J. 1994. "School Daze." Review of *City on a Hill: Testing the American Dream at City College*, by J. Traub. *The Nation* 259 (15): 522–28.

Wiengarten, S., and F. P. Kroeger, eds. 1965. *English in the Two-Year College*. Champaign, Ill: National Council of Teachers of English.

Wilentz, S. 1989. "The Rise of the Working Class, 1776–1877: A Survey." In *Perspectives on American Labor History: The Problems of Synthesis*, ed. J. C. Moody and A. Kesler-Harris, 83–151. DeKalb, Ill.: Northern Illinois University Press.

Willinsky, J. 1990. *The New Literacy: Redefining Reading and Writing in the Schools*. New York: Routledge.

Wisgoski, A. 1971. "Characteristics of Junior College Students: Implications for Faculty and Student Personnel Specialists." In *Perspectives on the Community-Junior College*, ed. W. K. Ogilvie and M. R. Raines, 183–89. New York: Merideth Corporation.

The Women of Summer. 1986. Prod. S. Bauman and R. Heller. 60 min. Filmmakers Library. Videocassette.

Zandy, J., ed. 1995. *Liberating Memory: Our Work and Our Working-Class Consciousness*. New Brunswick, N.J.: Rutgers University Press.

Zinn, H. 1980. *A People's History of the United States*. New York: Harper & Row.